The experts agree ....

.... every Ridgeback model exemplifies the very latest in purpose-made off-road technology. That's why experienced riders and critics agree, for the genuine mountain biking experience - you can't beat a Ridgeback.

66 It was the Ridgeback 603 I bought back in '86 that inspired me to go on to write a book on mountain biking **99**

Barry Ricketts (Author)
The Mountain Biking Handbook

66 We run all the major brands... Ridgebacks are ahead of the bunch for quality and ride performance **99**

John Stevenson (Manager)
Two Wheels Good : ATB specialists

66 In the off-season I use a Ridgeback to add an extra dimension to my winter training program **99**

Mark Walsham (Percy Bilton)
1988 Pro Criterium Champion

Competition Series 603

RIDGEBACK

For information and the address of your nearest authorised dealer telephone Madison Cycles on 01-452 5401.

NEW Deore XT[II]
The Total Control System

A new bench mark for ATB performance

Take on the challenge of high performance off-road cycling with Deore XT[II]. A product of Shimano's systems approach to component design, Deore XT[II] reflects the total accumulated know-how of Shimano off-road technology.

Deore XT[II] incorporates advanced new functions. **Hyperglide** sprockets make SIS shifting faster and smoother than ever. A new 7-speed gearing system provides a wider gear choice with famed **SIS** precision**.**

Biopace HP chainrings let you ride all-out with greatly increased pedalling efficiency. And the new **SLR** booster U-Brake/cantilever system delivers dynamic braking power with fingertip control.

This is the ultimate component system for off-roaders who just won't settle for second best. Deore XT[II]. The new bench mark in component design.

MUDDY FOX

The Mountain Bike People

BEWARE OF IMITATIONS

For your free colour guide to genuine mountain bikes and more
contact Muddy Fox at

Dept.MH• 331 Athlon Road • Wembley • Middlesex HA0 1BY • Telephone: 01-998 8711 (10 lines)

MUDDY FOX USA
3539 Haven Avenue
Menlo Park
California 94025
U.S.A.
Tel: (415) 364 5244
Toll-free
In state: 1-800 543 6996
Out of state: 1-800 942 6336
Fax: (415) 364 5248

MUDDY FOX U.K.
95 Manor Farm Road
Wembley
Middlesex
HA0 1BY
United Kingdom
Tel: 01 998 8711
Tx: 27421 MUDDY G
Fax: 01 991 5963

MUDDY FOX SWITZERLAND
Chemin de la Concorde 4
CH-2503 Bienne
Switzerland
Tel: 032 251544

MUDDY FOX BELGIUM
Brasseur
Rue des Steppes 13
4000 Liege
Belgium
Tel: 041 27 32 43
Tel: 041 27 68 00
Tx: 41116 BRASSR B

MUDDY FOX HOLLAND
P.O.Box 4922
2003EX Haarlem
Holland
Tel: 02508 1444
Tx: 28177 VABIX
Fax: 10 429 31 58

MUDDY FOX JAPAN
1-47 Fukushima 3-Chome
Fukushima-Ku
Osaka
Japan
Tel: 06 454-0785
Tx:J63586
Fax: 06 454 0230

Panaracer

DIA-COMPE

TANGE

SANSIN

Sugino

TANGE

ARAYA

SHIMANO

SUNTOUR

THE MOUNTAIN BIKING HANDBOOK

THE
MOUNTAIN
BIKING
HANDBOOK

BARRY RICKETTS

THE ARENA PRESS

THE ARENA PRESS
The Arena Press/Dalton Watson plc
Russell Chambers
The Piazza
Covent Garden
LONDON
WC2E 8AA

First published 1988

British Library Cataloguing in Publication Data

Ricketts, Barry
  The mountain biking handbook
  1. Mountainous regions. Cycling
  I. Title
  796.6'0914'3

  ISBN 1-85443-005-X

Designed and produced by ᵗʰᵉPEN & INK
BOOK CO LIMITED

Printed by Scotprint Ltd, Musselburgh, Scotland

PUBLISHER'S NOTE
Where brand names and manufacturers of mountain bikes and equipment are referred to or pictured in this book, such references are not intended to be endorsements of individual makes, nor should the omission of other brand names be taken as non-endorsement.

The Arena Press draws the reader's attention particularly to the section on 'Legal Access' on pages 100 – 101 of this book. It is the responsibility of the individual to check, before embarking on an off-road ride, that such a ride is not an infringement of laws or by-laws, by consulting the relevant authorities.

ACKNOWLEDGEMENTS
The studio photography in this book was produced by Colorific, Slough. Other photographs were kindly provided by Stephen Behr (pages 22, 32, 86–7), Geoff Waugh (14, 24 – top, 30–31, 45, 82, 100–101, 108, 109 – top), Nick Crane/Peter Inglis (21 and 149), Giles Smith (20) and Barry Ricketts.
The figures were drawn by R. Bonson, the maps by Frank Kennard and the cartoon by Dave Parkins.

We also thank various contributors of photographs which it has proved impossible to attribute individually – particularly the Cross-country Cycling Club and the British Cyclo-Cross Association. We are also grateful for the generous assistance of Madison Cycles plc, who provided equipment, people and much patient help in the studio and on location.

CONTENTS

BASICS

ENJOYING YOUR SPORT

SELF-SUFFICIENCY

The BMX bike, seen here competing over a mountain biking trials course, was one of the initial inspirations for the mountain bike

▶ INTRODUCTION ◀

The great joy of mountain biking, and probably the secret of its overwhelming international success, is the fact that it can mean many different things to its adherents, and all of them are valid.

To mountain bike purists, it is the out-and-out assault of rider and machine against the most extreme natural terrain. The grinding progress up near-vertical gradients, and the hair-raising, death-defying descents which wrest the last ounce of resilience and endurance from tortured metal and distorted tyre treads.

Another, esoteric breed of user can be seen in crowded city centres, astride the same machines, solving traffic snarls, taking granite steps and kerbs in their stride. They represent the species' ultimate adaptation to the mechanized paralysis of late-twentieth-century urbanization. To these bikers, their machine breaks the bonds of deadlocked traffic. So successfully does it accomplish this, that in New York and London the mountain bike courier is becoming even more ubiquitous than his motorcycling predecessor – an encouraging example of low-technology evolution.

To the kids progressing up from BMXs which so perfectly matched the exuberance of youth with a pair of wheels, the mountain bike is a natural transition – streetwise, macho, but traffic-safe and high-performance.

But more than this, examine any colourful sprawl of machines outside a cycling club's favourite haunt or watering place, and the chunky, fat-tyred, straight-handlebarred beasties will be well in evidence. The only difference between Dad and his small Sunday-riding brood will be wheel size. No cycle-shop window will be without a selection of prominently displayed bright-liveried mountain bikes.

The mount is the message – and it has been the renaissance of cycling. So much so that in less than ten years, the mountain bike has gone from freakish West Coast US phenomenon to the biggest-selling adult bicycle type in the US, Canada and (almost) the United Kingdom.

It has not merely supplanted sales of more conventional machines. It has brought cycling to a whole new range of consumers who never before included the sport or pastime in their lives.

Self-image-conscious yuppies twin Porsche and a mountain bike in their personal transportation portfolio. It is the preferred second sport of many of the international windsurfing set. Ridgewalkers are confronting the heretical machine and finding it extends their range and horizons. The middle-life fitness seeker, preferring scenery to bathroom ceramics, is increasingly in evidence on suburban bridleways. To kids (of all ages) mountain bikes are just the business!

Many keen cyclists have mountain bikes as their second bike, admiring the sophisticated componentry and rugged good looks which complement their other, racier example of the cyclemaker's art. The machine has found a place in the hearts of boys, girls, men and women from all social strata. It has done so because it combines mobility and style, brings a promise of freedom and the great outdoors and, above all other things, it has great character.

To the cycle trade, worldwide, the bike has been nothing short of an economic miracle. It has already made millionaires, and will go on to make more. To the enthusiast, it is an exhilarating new aspect of the sport. To the novice, it means access to places previously only dreamt about, or approached on foot, without the thrill of the dangerous descent. The commuter has experienced a quantum leap in efficiency and economy – even if the beneficial effects of exercise are neutralized by carbon monoxide and the ever present danger of other traffic.

Of course, no 'giant leap forward' is ever without its problems and disadvantages. Already, some environmentalists, and those who have long regarded the countryside as reserved for feet and hooves, have raised their voices against the sport. If this powerful threat is to be avoided, cyclists must become responsible sharers of the countryside and learn to care in word and deed for their environment.

The competitive side – trials, races and the like – is an essential part of the development of the sport, technically, socially and in terms of media awareness. This aspect has had a shaky beginning, and those organizing spirits who will guide it into a course which can benefit so many have yet to emerge.

So far, the overwhelming friendliness of the cyclist as a life-form has prevented the weird schisms which have disfigured other great transport enthusiasms – such as the rivalry between motorcyclists and scooterists – degenerating so often into violence. Long may the camaraderie of the true cyclist prevail.

The purpose of this book is to consolidate into one handy volume the mass of wise words, technical jargon and knowledge, history and lore, advice and instructions on how to get started, how to become proficient, enjoy, be good at, and become a credit to mountain biking.

A number of other writers and books stand behind the *Mountain Biking Handbook*. All are acknowledged, and all are unreservedly recommended to the enthusiast. Without those earlier works, this compilation of what is currently known and relevant could not have been produced.

Few other sports, save perhaps windsurfing, microlite flying and one or two other obscure but delightful passions, can be documented at a time when the originators, key influencers and most notable performers are all at the peak of their powers. So fast has been the growth of the mountain bike, as a machine and as a movement, that this is definitely the case in the late 1980s. We have tried to include all the prime influences and personalities in this book, but it is inevitable that history will continue to be written in the sport as you, the reader, turn the pages. The charm and challenge which this sport offers is that it could be you making that history.

BASICS

History can be a poor record of fact. All too often, writers and historians attempt to identify a single date or event which alone denotes the starting point of a subject. Nowhere is this more true than with mountain biking, since most commentators would have their readers believe that the sport and the machines evolved during a sudden, seemingly spontaneous, burst of activity in Marin County, California, during the 1970s.

That Marin County, and more specifically a forest hill-trail known as the 'Repack', played a major role in the development of the American-style mountain bike is undoubtedly true. Without the mountain bike – a unique blend of innovative American and far-eastern engineering, organization and marketing hype – the sudden international surge of interest in off-road cycling that has occurred in the last ten years would have been impossible. But the early mountain bikes careered on to

a stage already criss-crossed by the tyre tracks of many an all-terrain biker.

The desire to ride rough tracks, to take the bicycle where other vehicles cannot penetrate, even to compete on courses so primitive that the bike has to be carried as much as ridden, has been with the cycling fraternity for many years.

The first Cyclo-Cross event was held in France in 1902, and now the sport takes place in all the European and most British Commonwealth countries. The major international events are often televised and attract valuable prize money and sponsorship.

In Britain, the Cyclists' Touring Club has been in existence since 1878, and records many an intrepid ride off the beaten track. More significantly, the 'Rough Stuff Fellowship', formed in 1955 with the specific purpose of promoting the sport of riding bicycles on tracks, byways and out of the way

Cyclo-Cross is still a thriving sport

places, documents many an ascent of high Alpine summits, many a traverse of uncharted terrain.

The desire to break new ground – or at the very least escape from the constant noise, pollution and danger of modern traffic and pedal into the world's lonelier, lovelier places – touches almost every cyclist at times. Many have converted their vague longings into more tangible projects and expeditions, and their exploits are recorded later in this book.

The very act of taking the bike off metalled roads and on to rough terrain implies the acquisition of new riding skills, and this appeals immediately to the competitive spirit. Mountain biking is not far from the heart of every schoolchild; little formal organization is required before an eager group of cyclists will pit their machines and skills against each other on a rubble-strewn waste plot.

Of course, the 'BMX' was a direct appeal to this youthful desire, owing much, admittedly, to trials and dirt-track motorbikes in design and style. Nonetheless, it too has had an important influence on the development of the more purist sport of mountain biking.

What cannot be denied is that during the eighties a disjointed, informal, wholly unofficial pastime evolved into one of the world's newest, most successful adventure sports. As a side effect, it regenerated the bicycle and accessory industry, created whole new markets in functional and fashionable goods, and brought the energy, glamour and flair of windsurfing and skydiving into cycling.

The influence of Repack Hill, Marin County, has been crucial in the development of technology, and in attracting the new breed of sportsmen and women for whom risk, glamour and expensive state-of-the-art equipment are a vital ingredient to their enjoyment. By nature, these people are trend-setters and communicators, and it was their dedicated myth-making and entre-preneurial drive that took semi-legal back-country dirt-tracking into the international big-time. Once the nucleus of a new sport was there, it was eagerly embraced by the millions of dedicated cyclists world-wide, who were ready for an injection of new excitement and equipment into their sport.

So what is Repack, and who are the people who are forging the latest in a long list of cycling legends?

In California in the late 60s–early 70s, the state was experiencing difficulty with groups of local youngsters who, having graduated from BMX bikes to trials motorcycles, were tearing up the local countryside by climbing to the top of mountain trails and firebreaks in forested country, and proceeding to the bottom by the fastest, often most dangerous routes.

Inevitably, many rural citizens were offended by the noise, environmental damage and hazard to other country-side users, and a statewide ban ensued. However, in Marin County, where from one point of view 'the problem' had been particularly acute, from another 'the sport' particularly strong, the young enthusiasts applied their minds to the problem, and began to take to the hills on wheels powered by legs rather than internal combustion.

The frail ten-speed road-racing machines which constituted the top-selling bikes in the US at the time were clearly unsuited to the mountain tracks down which they plummeted, so the riders began to scour second-hand dealers, cellars and barns to find the sturdy roadsters of an earlier era. By the mechanical version of Darwin's process of natural selection, the machine which rapidly rose to become the dominant species was the Schwinn Excelsior – ideally from the vintage produced from 1933 to the early 40s – equipped with balloon tyres, 'coaster' hub brakes and wide, upswept handlebars. This vener-able relic was no lightweight, but what it lacked in portability, it more than compensated for in rugged inde-structibility; an essential characteristic, for the Californian hill trails were becoming famous for their ability to 'total' almost any component on any bike which regularly descended them at speed.

Most famous among these mountain track bike-breakers was the Cascades fire road on Mt. Tamalpais. So steep was this fierce descent that any rider fortunate enough to stay aboard his flying Schwinn to the bottom would find that he had boiled off the grease in his coaster brakes, which would then have to be 'repacked' before another descent was attempted. The legend was born. Now, the Cascades is officially renamed 'Repack Hill', and the birthplace of the moutain bike provided not only the first truly recognized and documented performance records in the new sport, but was the nursery from which sprang the names and equipment which have now become internationally renowned.

If the flying Schwinn was the ideal projectile to jockey down Repack's average 1 in 7 two-mile switchback, it was far from ideal as a means of transport up the hill. Riders would assemble at the bottom to wait for a pickup truck to return them to the top for a second descent. It took Garry Fisher, fastest man ever in the 'Repack Race', and a road-racing cyclist to boot, to fit gears to the old battle charger, and make the first unassisted ascent of Repack on a Schwinn.

By this time, mountain biking was attracting a lot of attention, and the American passion for customizing equipment was bound to take hold. One of Garry Fisher's cycling rivals, Joe Breeze, first analysed the success of the Schwinn and diagnosed the angles, rather than sheer weight, as the magic ingredient in the veteran 'clunker's' downhill virtuosity. Breeze was a fairly experienced framebuilder, having taken a course in the art run by the US maestro, Albert Eisentraut, and had already built a number of road frames. In 1977, in response to requests from fellow Repackers, Garry built ten frames, substituting large diameter Chrome Moly tubing for the mild steel Schwinn originals; incorporating the

gearing and quick-release adjustable seat posts innovated by Fisher, but mimicking the laidback angles of the Schwinn. Those frames are still in use today!

The first bikes sported a 44 inch wheelbase, 68° head tube and 70° seat. More importantly, they sliced pounds from the all-up weight of the bike, and at last the beast climbed as well as she dived!

It is important to note that back in 1953, a maker called John Finley Scott had built an off-road bike on a Schwinn frame that bore a strong resemblance to today's mountain bikes, but the venture was premature. Clearly, the stimulus of downhill bike racing was crucial to the development of the market.

If a culture of near-suicidal downhill racing was essential to the sport in

America, an entirely different spirit prevailed in the UK and the rest of Europe. Here, cycling was more a utilitarian pastime, with many people relying on their bikes for essential daily transport. In the US, bikes have always been regarded as a fun or sporting object; in Europe, they transport millions to school, work, into the country for weekend pleasure rides (or, for the more serious, time-trials and road races).

Indeed, in France, Italy and Spain, racing cyclists are highly paid professionals, idolized as sports megastars

Tough but not indestructible – abuse will damage even a mountain bike. The amount of force required to straighten the bent forks shows the inherent strength of the materials used

and paid salaries to match. Against such an established cycling background, who needed a fringe American import – either the sport, or the machines?

Cycling off-road was not unknown. There were even specialist makers who catered for the aesthetes of the 'Rough Stuff Fellowship' in Britain, with designers like Geoff Apps producing such machines as the 'Range Rider' in the late 70s. This machine, developed first by Jeremy Torr and latterly by Dave Wrath-Sharman, survives as the 'Highpath' esteemed by some British connoisseurs as the ultimate mountain bike.

But the esoteric few who pedalled the high passes were not the thousands who would flock to the mountain bike, and the domestic cycle industry, ruefully rubbing wounds after the early demise of the BMX craze, eschewed the

brash new American arrivals. They could not have been more wrong.

Despite the lack of sophisticated marketing campaigns or any great following in the media, the new bikes began to be seen around. They showed up on top of mountains at home and abroad, crossed deserts, set new records for distance and endurance, and began to create a following of dedicated trend-setters.

The machines themselves were largely American designed, Japanese or Taiwanese built and equipped – at least in the early days. Despite a long tradition of cycle building in Europe, the major manufacturers almost entirely overlooked the new development, dismissing it as a craze, and thus coming late to the biggest bike party since dropped handlebars and high-pressure tyres put the race-leader's yellow jersey firmly in the sights of every schoolchild. But now, just ten short years after it assumed its current form, the mountain bike is everywhere. It knows no age limit, no social niche, and apparently no boundaries to growth, either in its burgeoning popularity as a sport or its commercial success.

Today, in Britain alone, there are a dozen or more 'national' events for mountain bikes, and some 80,000 individual machines were in use at the time of writing. It is estimated this will double within the year. Wherever you live in the country, you are close to a dealer who will provide you with a representative sample of the best hardware; and if the choice is limited, there is a well-established and efficient mail order industry to fill the gap. Several framebuilders will custom-make your dreambike and the catalogues of all major manufacturers sport one or more models to suit most budgets.

The Mountain Bike Club is a thriving young organization, and its founders and members are ever eager to advise the novice or experienced rider. The mountain bike is here, and every indication is that it will carve out a place for itself in the world of cycling, for pleasure, competition and work, that will endure for many years.

In the beginning, mountain bikes were uncompromising two-wheeled down-hill slalom machines. Then, within a few years, the concept developed to the point where, today, the mountain bike is the dominant cycle species, equally at home in Snowdonia or Sloane Street, San Francisco or the Sahara.

Defining the essential machine is difficult. Frames and accessories are changing rapidly, to such an extent that it is impossible to fix the specification to any set formula. A number of character-istics prevail. Mountain bikes have larger tyres than other bikes – 1.5 to 2.25 inches is the normal range – but they may be heavily treaded (knobbly) or smooth, depending on the terrain covered by the rider. Frame size is generally 2 to 2.5 inches smaller than the equivalent road bike for the same rider – smaller frames tend to be stronger and are lighter. Frames are usually of high-specification alloy steel – though some notable exceptions have aluminium/steel, even carbon-fibre/steel or aluminium combinations – and the other metal parts are almost exclusively light alloy.

Even those specifications don't pre-cisely define the mountain bike, for, with the exception of tyres and rim size, the description could apply readily to bikes which fall outside the category.

At the time of writing, the classic design has a triangulated, or diamond frame, similar to that found on conven-tional road bikes, but adapted for all-terrain use. The frame is the heart of a machine which must be capable of climbing the steepest gradient, de-scending rugged terrain at high speed, ploughing through mud, sand or snow without becoming clogged up and immobilized, yet light enough to be carried over those parts of the route impossible to scale on a bike.

The feats of the Crane cousins – Nick and Richard – demonstrate the extremes to which the mountain bike can be taken. In the early 1980s, when the first machines began to appear in Britain, they took a pair of the machines up the 'Fourteen Peaks' in the Black Mountains

Richard and Nick Crane ascending one of the fourteen peaks of Snowdonia

of Wales. The peaks, much beloved of rock climbers, are all over 3,000 feet, and many are almost vertical faces normally attempted by roped and belayed teams. Imagine, then, the dismay of such a team as they were passed on a pitch by two sweating cyclists, in too much of a hurry to rope up, and 'portaging' the mountain bikes over their shoulders. 'At times', writes Crane in his hilarious book *The Great Bicycle Adventure*, 'the bikes were an encumbrance: they tended to jam in chimneys and threaten to topple us from narrow ledges.'

So, to get to the places their more ambitious riders want to take them, mountain bikes must be light. To withstand the hammering they will undoubtedly receive once they get there, they must be strong to the point of virtual indestructibility.

Such an exacting specification demands outstanding materials, brilliant design and high build quality. There can be no doubt that the better makes

combine all these things, but you get what you pay for, so it's necessary to be very clear-minded about the type of riding you will be doing before you buy your bike (see pages 29–36).

Increasingly, the machine is to be seen on city streets. This is not just because its 'ready for anything' good looks make it a natural for the urban poseur; the bike is eminently suited to weaving through matted traffic in a fraction of the time taken by any other form of transport, and as roads throughout Britain and America deteriorate as a result of dwindling city funding, so the 'all terrain bicycle' becomes a more durable proposition than its distant cousin, the fragile street racer. The geometry of the mountain bike absorbs shocks more easily – with a little skill, riding up and down steps is perfectly possible – the head-up position induced by straight or upswept handlebars is safer, and the big tyres (smooth-treaded for city use) and more ample saddles iron out the bumps as if the machine were equipped with hydraulic suspension.

The mountain bike is that great rarity, a perfect compromise. With a little adaptation, the same machine will propel you to work in the heart of the city, hurtle headlong down a mountainside in a timed 'suicide slalom' event, or take you expeditioning in Arctic or Equatorial regions. All you do is change tyres, add or subtract such items as panniers and mudguards, and make sure your cholera shots are up to date!

Most vital is the **frame**, for it supports the weight of the rider and provides the fixing-points for all other essential equipment. Most of the frames available today derive from the basic designs of Californian Joe Breeze, who first married the geometry of the 'cruiser' bikes of an earlier age with light, high-tensile steel tubing and scientifically advanced construction techniques, and pushed the prototype over a Marin County mountainside.

By far the majority of frames are constructed in Japan or Taiwan, with even large UK manufacturers such as Raleigh importing stock for subsequent assembly in individual markets. Of course, some domestic manufacturers in the US and Europe (including Raleigh) make at least some of their own output, but these are largely confined to the premium end of the range, since the build quality, value for money and material content of the far-eastern product is hard to beat.

Steel alloys are the predominant tubing material, with some exotic machines employing aluminium in part or in whole, and a very few introducing such space-age materials as carbon-fibre and Kevlar. The steel tubing used is alloyed with chromium, molybdenum or manganese, and is drawn to a greater thickness at the ends (butted) in order to increase joint strength – although this means sacrificing the minimum lightness.

Some frames are joined with cast steel lugs, socketed angle pieces which exactly accept the ends of the frame tubes to form the final frame design; others are welded or brazed together without the use of lugs. This second technique is more common for mountain bikes because of the preference for oversize tubes and varying tube profiles, which add strength to specific parts of the frame. Good makes of frame are made of such materials as 'Cro-Mo' tubing, Reynolds 531 or 501, Tange, Ishiwata, Columbus or Vitus. Some machines, especially those hand-crafted by the specialized small frame-maker, and accessible to a few fortunate bike nuts (or those prepared to survive on nuts to afford a state-of-the-art frame!), combine materials – for instance, forks in Reynolds 531, and frame in Columbus tubing. Some American bikes – and the US still innovates in the field – are 'rifled', which means they are internally ribbed in a spiral which travels in the opposite direction to the torque forces, so resisting the strains imposed by pedalling.

A distinctive feature of the mountain bike frame is the fork crown, the point where the blades which pinion the front wheel are connected to the tube which turns within the 'head' or 'steering' tube of the frame. This is a point of great stress in comparison with bikes whose main business is transacted on tarmac, and the construction must be rugged enough to take head-on encounters with granite boulders! Wrap-around braze or weld joints, often with the additional strength endowed by lugs, is the order of the day here.

Other frame features which distinguish the true mountain bike include custom 'braze-ons' and fork ends. The former are fittings which precisely anchor such equipment as brakes, cables and gear mechanisms, ensuring positive location at all times; the latter are slotted plates at the end of the front and rear forks which hold the wheel hub axles and which, in the case of rear wheels, may be dedicated to a particular type of derailleur gear-shifting mechanism.

Frame geometry, the angles and relationships between the main tubes and stays of the bike, have an effect both on ride – 'stiff' or 'soft' quick steering and responsive, slower steering and 'forgiving' – and on the practical performance of the machine. For instance, a low bottom-bracket means greater stability, but less ground clearance; a short wheelbase gives better climbing ability but less downhill stability at speed. There is no such thing as the ideal frame geometry, simply because no two riders are alike. Manufacturers tend to make the compromises for us, and their choices are fairly predictable, with the bigger manufacturer going for the safe design, tending towards touring bikes, while the smaller, specialized makers carry more extreme race-developed frames in their range.

Few of the high-volume makers offer down-sloping top-tubes and ultra-short chainstays in combination with very out-of-parallel seat- and head-tubes.

Oversize tubes, all-welded construction and a distinctive, often reinforced fork crown characterize many mountain bike frames

That sort of machine would be more at home in a severe observed trial or hill climb than touring in the Cotswolds or Catskills.

Of course, none of this means that the more extreme frame designs cannot be used for street riding, nor that a well-prepared tourer will not – in the right hands – win competitions. But, if you want something different, you have to pay the price. On pages 40-47 you will find more detail on frame design and selection.

The equipment that accompanies the frame has come full circle since the days when pioneer mountain bikers scavenged parts from other types of cycle and adapted them to their riding needs. Indeed, so successful has the genre become as a means of testing components (often to destruction), that equipment has been improved for all types of machines. Significantly, all the main manufacturers now include at least one 'ATB range'*of parts in their catalogues, and any serious machine must feature such equipment to perform its task.

Wheels are the next most important item after the frame. They must be of light alloy, and of a strong construction, capable of taking tyres from around 1.5 to 2.25 inches. The standard wheel size on mountain bikes is 26 inches, although some machines employ 24-inch wheels, and a mix of 26-inch front and 24-inch rear is not unknown on competition machinery.

The principal advantage of alloy over steel is weight. On a bicycle, revolving weight is even more important than the static variety, since centrifugal forces tend to increase its effect. Alloy rims and hubs are a considerable saving in revolving weight, and no serious mountain bike will carry steel in either of these vital functions.

Rear wheels are built with a dished hub and spoking arrangement on the offside (right side) of the wheel. This means that the side where the rear sprockets of the gearing system are carried is flatter than the other side of

The Cannondale competition machine with 24-inch rear wheel

the wheel, to allow sufficient room for a block of five or six (or even seven on the more extreme versions) sprockets to be mounted on the rear hub. Theoretically, this form of wheelbuilding is less strong than a perfectly symmetrical pattern; in practice, the wheels survive remarkable punishment before signs of distress appear.

Hubs can be large- or small-flanged, according to taste. There is a trade-off here between the greater strength of a large-flanged hub and the reduced weight of the smaller variety. Spokes enter the larger-flanged hubs at a more acute angle, and this can be a cause of breakage, but such considerations are really esoteric, and selection tends to be governed more by opinion and taste

*ATB. Just to confuse us, some manufacturers and marketing departments have adopted the term 'all terrain bicycle' – ATB – for the mountain bike, presumably to capture sales in such bicycle-mad, but mountainless, countries as the Netherlands. Where the term is used in this book, it should be taken to mean mountain bike.

QR front hub

than science. More quick-release hub mechanisms are appearing on mountain bikes these days, and they appear to work quite well, offering an advantage of convenience over the traditional wheel nut, with no apparent loss of safety.

Tyres are arguably the most important component, and it is puzzling to see how many riders seem to be prepared to spend a small fortune on the 'shiny bits', only to sport worn, or

The Shimano XT range of equipment

inappropriate, tyres. There are three main types of 'shoe' for your mount: out-and-out off-road competition tyres; 'all-surface' tyres, knobbly enough to give fair traction off-road, but with a raised continuous centre band to give less rolling resistance on tarmac; and smooth or semi-smooth 'fatties' for the street machine. These all vary in width and tread pattern, and are dealt with in detail on pages 59–60.

Saddles and steering gear are often the most distinctive features. There are two schools of thought on the matter of seating: sprung, broad seats for the machine spending most time off-road; contoured 'anatomical' varieties for the mixed road and bridlepath rider. One feature developed for the mountain bike, quick-release seat pillars to allow rapid adjustment of saddle height, also permits rapid removal, allowing the really well-equipped rider both options.

Sprung and unsprung saddle designs

Upswept or straight handlebars made from aluminium and attached to the bike via upward tilting stems are the norm, although a few rare racers and one stock machine from Muddy Fox sport dropped handlebars.

The bars, as well as supporting the rider and playing a major role in navigation, are the point of attachment for the controls: thumb-shifter levers for the gear-changing mechanisms, and the front and rear brake levers. Some manufacturers now combine these assemblies.

The controls connect with their business ends via Bowden cables, routed along frame tubes by strategically placed brazed-on guides. This means of fixing avoids the movement and weight associated with bolt or clip-on guides. At the end of the brake cables are the **brakes**. The usual front brake arrangement is a centre-pull cantilever, the left and right parts of which pivot on brazed bosses mounted on the front of each

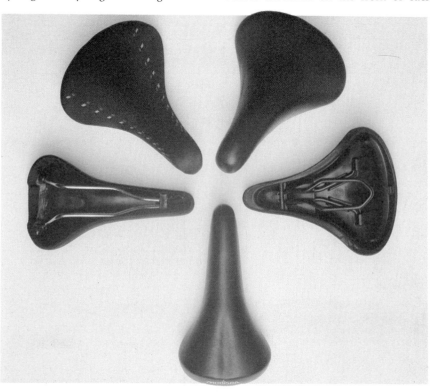

fork blade. The design, developed for tandems, is extremely efficient, especially when combined with the superior braking qualities of alloy rims. The rear brake can have a similar arrangement, with the pivots mounted on the seat stays just below the cross-member, or a 'U-brake' mounted beneath the chainstay, where an alloy yoke forms the mounting for two levers which apply the brake blocks to the rim. For mountain bikes, top-quality composite brake blocks should be used, and replaced regularly if you value life and limb.

Gearing, or **transmission**, is one of the features which sets apart the mountain bike from other machinery. First, there is much more of it – fifteen to eighteen ratios are normal, twenty-one possible. The wide spread and number of ratios and gears is achieved by a rear derailleur shifting the chain over a freewheel mechanism carrying from five to seven sprockets, and a triple chainwheel, with a front derailleur mounted above the chainwheels on the seat tube of the bike. While based on the same systems as those in use on normal ten-speed road bikes, the moun-

tain bike variant is much tougher, and capable of handling the far bigger rear sprockets and smaller front chainrings necessary to obtain the ultra-low gears which power mountain bikes up seemingly impossible gradients. Chainrings drive rear sprockets via a chain and, in the case of mountain bikes, top-quality narrow chains (changed frequently) are essential.

Again, light alloys are used extensively in the construction of this machinery, although it is mixed with some of the exotic high-strength materials like titanium, and other products of the aerospace industry, to achieve the mixture of strength and lightness essential to survival of components in the field.

Pedals are usually of the 'beartrap' variety, with strong construction to withstand occasional grounding, and serrated edges to give cleated soles something to cling on to in the absence of toe clips. Some mountain bikers fit clips to their pedals, and for some events that provides an undeniable edge. It depends on your enthusiasm for following your bike over every crevasse; there are those riders who will

wish to retain some element of choice in this matter!

That is the basic specification of the mountain bike, as it has evolved at the time of writing. Obviously, other components can be fitted, and popular options are mudguards and panniers, both specially adapted to the wide, high clearances necessary. Lights may be required, but attachment will be via tough plastic clips to allow the complete removal of the lights before taking to the country. Failure to remove them will almost certainly result in their loss on the first serious encounter with the environment.

Choosing a mountain bike isn't simply a case of selecting the machine whose colour and general looks appeal to the eye. Nor will a sparkling specification and a ruinous price tag be the best guide to satisfaction. The most important job is to decide what function your mountain bike will perform in your life.

▶FIRST-TIME RIDER◀

In many ways the easiest need to meet is that of the first-time 'big bike' user. Usually a young boy or girl moving up from a junior cycle, such a rider will probably have had some experience of the BMX bike, and will want to combine the freedom and fun of these delightful machines with a serious bike for use in traffic, as well as for charging over the nearest farm track.

This category of rider is well catered for by all the large manufacturers, and

A full range of accessories and parts is available to help you suit your bike to your needs

the prime consideration is to get good value for money in the genuine article, and not be fooled by a glossy imitation which turns out to lack the basic attributes which qualify it for the term 'mountain bike'.

Obviously, one of the most important factors is budget, and this is often quite restricted when you are buying a bike for a growing child. Brothers and sisters may also have needs; early teenage is anyway an expensive time, and there may be a suspicion that the child will outgrow, or even tire of, cycling.

The answer is to go for as versatile and high-quality a machine as possible. Easily said, but how are the non-technical to judge the quality of something as specialized as a mountain bike? Here are some guidelines.

▶Size◀

As a rule of thumb, mountain bikes are smaller-framed than touring or so-called 'racing' bikes. This is a useful weight saving, and smaller frames are also stronger, and lower crossbars or top

tubes less dangerous in a fall. Of course, the suitability of the smaller frame does mean that, for the growing youngster, the ATB will be performing a useful job for longer.

However, a word of warning – not every cycle shop can break the habit of sizing customers up as if for road bikes, so check the measurements for yourself. There should be up to 4 inches between the top tube and the crotch when the rider is standing astride the bike with both feet flat on the ground. It is as well to have a good inch of seat pillar protruding from the frame – this will allow for some 6 to 8 inches upwards growth, and that is a lot in teenage. As the child progresses, seat fixings with more rearwards movement can be fitted, as can longer handlebar stems. As long as you have bought a good frame from a reliable manufacturer, it will perform very well through the useful life of the bike. Indeed, for many riders, the same size of mountain bike frame will last them all their riding life.

▶ Materials and construction ◀

'A good frame from a reliable manufacturer' can mean several things. To youngsters, fashion will play a big part, and the heavily advertised machines, such as Muddy Fox, Dawes, Peugeot, Specialized and Raleigh, will be high on their list. This is no bad thing, since such international companies have reputations to preserve, and will usually build a reliable product in the first place, and then operate a reasonable guarantee, given reasonable use. (Of course, mountain bikes and youngsters are almost a recipe for abuse, but the general state of a bike will be taken into account when they assess a claim.) Perhaps the best guarantee of quality is in the construction of the **frame**.

The section on frames on pages 40-47 explains in detail the types of alloy steel, and the joining methods employed. The products of all the above-mentioned manufacturers are reliable in all their various price ranges. Obviously, the ultra-light high-alloy steel machines will

Make sure a reputable steelmaker's transfer complements the pretty paint job

be at the top of the price range, and the quality of materials and construction methods will decrease as the price descends, but a machine from the lower-to-medium-price end of any of these stables is a good starting-point for a new rider.

The thing to avoid is a frame which carries no steel-maker's transfer. Reynolds, Tange, Colombus, Cro-Mo, Carbolite and so on are all good; such terminology as 'Hi-Ten Steel' suggests a less suitable material. This doesn't mean that a perfectly serviceable bike cannot be produced in such materials, simply that it may be relatively heavy, and rather less responsive and sprightly in use. Over time, both the performance and prestige gaps will be noticed by any bright youngster, and a 'trade-up' will be desired. Given the long life expectancy of the frame, you might as well get the purchase right from the outset,

Given that the frame and wheels are of good quality on the first-time rider's machine, other components can be subject to sensible compromise, depending on the purpose to which it is to be put, and the budget available. The great delight of the bicycle is the interchangeability of parts, so 'upgrades' to almost any level are possible at whatever pace you pocket allows.

If, as is most likely to be the case, the cycle is to be the main form of transport, as well as a viable ATB, then a number of choices follow.

Tyres

The best type of tyre for such a general-purpose machine will be around 1.5 inches in width, having a raised, smooth central band and heavier tread on the shoulder of the tyre. If your 'rough terrain' will be kerbstones, potholes and the challenge of urban rough stuff rather than the more agricultural/rural surface, then one of the smoother 'slick' treads will give better service and comfort. The adhesion is in the rubber itself, and the purpose of the knobbly bits on the tread is to gain traction on uneven surfaces, by presenting greater surface area on gravel, sand or soil. On tarmac, the greater surface area is actually presented by a smoother tyre, and noise level is lower, while grip is as good as, if not better than, that of an off-road tyre.

Surprisingly, tyre tread plays a very small part in muddy conditions, for within a short time the mud has so clogged the tread that the tyre is practically 'slick' anyway.

since almost any other component is cheaper to replace.

Frame geometry is of low significance at this end of the market; most machines which qualify have fairly gentle 'laid-back' frames which will handle well off-road, and absorb the shocks of dilapidated paving in street riding.

Of the other materials and construction priorities, **wheels** are the most important. First, size. If you are of small stature, or buying for someone of small stature, Specialized supply a delightful high-spec machine with 24-inch wheels that is in every sense a full mountain bike, which will suit many girls, as well as young boys or, given the small frame requirement, smaller men. The most important feature of wheels, however, is that at least the rims should be of light alloy. This is particularly true for young riders, since weight is of prime importance to them, and wet steel rims make a very bad braking surface compared with the aluminium variety.

Handlebars

If you're planning mainly urban riding, the bars should be less wide than for a full off-road machine. An inch or so off the end of each bar is all it takes to get that extra bit of access in tight traffic conditions that makes all the difference. This is an adjustment that can be easily made for you by your dealer, on the stock bike you select.

Mudguards

There is no denying that the stripped-down mountain bike looks very raunchy. But in town, in rain, it does little for the image and less for the clothing. In fact, in a real downpour, the lack of adequate spray protection can be dangerous. Given the present fashion for rear brakes mounted beneath the chainstays, mudguards prevent at least some of the accumulation of gunge impeding the efficiency of the brake. Make sure that an ATB intended for commuting or urban living has adequate clearance to fit suitable guards, and if you are buying a new machine from a shop, get them dealer-fitted.

Ancillary equipment

Panniers and lights are a must for a machine called upon to be a jack of all trades to its rider. A pannier bag is useful, especially for school books and sports kit, and both Karrimor and Carradice make bags which are easily detachable, and which convert into rucksacks.

Any machine intended for general use ought to be capable of giving a good account of itself both on- and off-road, and there is no reason why the rest of

the equipment should not be genuine, uncompromising mountain bike gear. This is particularly true of such items as gearing, which, with an eighteen-ratio set, can be wide enough to cope with all gradients.

Brakes too, should be excellent, whatever the intended final use, and here most manufacturers wisely refuse to compromise. Look for a well-known brand. Although they are not the only acceptable names, Shimano, Suntour, Dia Compe and Weinmann are all proven makes.

If you follow these guidelines, and discuss your purchase with a dealer prepared to give you time and patience, you will be well suited, most likely with a stock machine from the lower to middle range of one of the major manufacturer's catalogues. The mountain bike you get may not be state-of-the-art, but it will be reliable, safe and open to a degree of up-rating at a later date. You will find this kind of machine for between £275 and £300.

▶URBAN STREET STOMPER◀

This is one of the more interesting sub-species of ATB and rider, since it has proved particularly apt for traffic conditions in modern cities, and has spawned a flourishing business – the mountain bike courier.

Quite early in the life of the mountain bike, urban youth saw the potential in a machine able to ride up and down kerbs and granite steps, cut across car parks and weave in and out of traffic with dexterity and speed. In many big cities, competitions from point to point between mountain bikes and any other form of transport imaginable have been held; the result invariably shows the clear superiority of the bike, Many new courier firms are able to cut days off the delivery time required for letters and small packages by the conventional mails. A hybrid mountain bike derivative has developed, equally at home as courier, student steed, time-share tool

for tourists, or home-to-office commute for the city-dweller.

▶Frame◀

Once again, the frame has priority and the same constraints as for other users will apply where materials and construction are concerned. Shock absorbency matters on today's care-worn urban roads, and lightness, too, counts. The machine may well have to be carried, especially if you live in a high-rise and know that the first time your bike stays on the street all night will be the last time you see it. A real aficionado will select a frame with slightly more erect geometry, to make for faster steering round obstacles and other traffic; the need for a very high bottom-bracket is not so acute.

▶Security◀

Sadly, one of the most important considerations for this type of machine has to be security. The advent of the mountain bike has stimulated a resurgence of the almost forgotten practice of bicycle theft, and in a society where the police can seldom find time to prosecute auto-theft efficiently, what chance does the humble bike stand?

It is essential to have one of the really substantial high U-bar security locks (such as Citadel), made in specially hardened steel, with a really ambitious seven-cylinder lock to shackle frame, rear wheel and detached front wheel to a railing or post. Riders who need to lock their bikes many times a day in this manner will tape the frame to prevent paint chipping and denting. Fit or specify a QR mechanism to the front wheel to allow speedy removal and replacement, and ensure that the seat post does not have a QR device, so that the saddle stands some chance of remaining with the rest of the machine. All other parts of the machine should be really securely attatched, and notices announcing that this 'Loctite Special' has all bolts double-secured with super-glue are not uncommon.

▶ ALL-ROUNDER ◀

There will be those users who expect rather more from the machine in terms of its off-road performance, perhaps intending to use it for fairly long and regular off-road excursions, maybe touring, and possibly the occasional novice race...even – as time progresses – more serious competition. Here the choices are far more diverse, and you're confronted with a price range from £375 to £500. The better Muddy Foxes, Ridgebacks, Specializeds, Raleighs and Dawes are the stock off-the-peg machines which spring immediately to mind, but they are representative of a level of excellence, rather than exclusive of other makes.

A specification which includes a good alloy steel frame, all-aluminium components, one of the middle to top range group-component sets from Suntour or Shimano, a fairly conventional diamond-type frame, with geometry ranging from 70° parallel to 68/73°, and all-up weights around the 30 lb-mark, will typify the lower to middle band of this range. At the higher end of the market, up to 3 lb will be shaved off the weight, framesets will include aluminium, and names such as Cannondale, Overbury's and Saracen will be in evidence. This is the real thing, just one step away from having your own made-to-measure frame, and you will certainly be buying a machine which will be equal to any task you call upon it to perform. And you won't even have to sacrifice a measure of versatility in your search for excellence. This machine can still be loaded with panniers, equipped with mudguards, and romp through a tour with the same panache that it brings to a weekend trial of mixed off-road competition in the Chilterns.

You would be well advised not to use this level of machinery for commuting or simple posing. Someone is likely to relieve you of your pride and joy the moment your train rolls out of the station, and that would be a great shame!

The Highpath – a unique British bike with a very full spec

▶ What you get for your money ◀

A selection of bikes across the price spectrum – extracted from a price survey listing more than ninety models, in *Mountain Biker*, September 1988.

The chart gives a very rough idea of what you should be able to expect in the various price bands when you choose your machine, and the capability that will give you in terms of everyday use and competition. Remember the golden rule – *always buy the best frame and wheels you can afford*. They will shine through, even when equipped with relatively cheap components, and you will be able gradually to improve the specification in time.

Price	Make/ Model	Frame Tubing and Design	Gears/ Shifters	Chainset/ Pedals	Hubs/ Rims	Tyres/ Brakes	Handlebars/ Saddle
£275	ORBIT	Reynolds 531c	Shimano LA	Solida triple	Alloy solid axle	26 × 1.75	Alloy
	Frontier 501		Thumbshifters	ATB	Alloy	Alloy cantilever	San Manatom
£375	BRITISH EAGLE	Reynolds 531 CS	Suntour Accushift 12 sp	Stronglight 100	Maillard	Specialized	ITM
	12sp ATB		Indexed	Lyotard	Weinmann	Shimano cant	Isca
£475	CINELLI	Columbus Cromar	Shimano Exage	Shimano Exage Mt	Shimano Exage	Kenda ATB	Cinelli
	Sentiero		SIS	Shimano Exage Mt	Araya	Shimano Exage	Cinelli
£580	SWALLOW	Reynolds 531 ATB, fillet-brazed lugless	Shimano Exage	Shimano Exage Mt	Shimano Exage	Specialized	Swallow
	Ptarmigan Exage		SIS	Shimano Exage Mt	Mavic Oxygene	Shimano Exage	Cinelli OR
£675	HOLDS-WORTH	Reynolds 531 lugged, with Tange Unicrown forks	Shimano Deore XT	Shimano Deore XT	Shimano Deore	Panaracer	SR
	Cape Wrath		SIS	Shimano Deore XT	Araya RM-20	Deore XT cant	Specialized
£765	FISHER	Aluminium and chromoly/ composite	Suntour XCD	Suntour XCD	Shimano Deore	Panaracer	Fisher bars
	Composite		Accushift	Suntour XCD	Araya RM-20	Suntour XCD	Avocet Touring
£860	CANNON-DALE	Welded oversize aluminium with Tange chromoloy forks	Shimano Deore Xt	Shimano Deore Xt	Shimano Deore	IRC racer	Alloy
	SM 1000		SIS	Shimano Deore XT	Araya RM-20	Shimano Deore	Turbo
£1075	EDINBURGH	Tange Prestige chromoly, fillet-brazed	Shimano Deore XT	Shimano Deore XT	Shimano Deore	Specialized	Specialized
	Cuillin		SIS	Shimano Deore XT	Araya RM-20	Shimano Deore	Madison

▶ TOP OF THE TREE ◀

At the very top of the tree comes the really serious competitor, for whom a highly specialized machine is required. Such a rider will already be a committed cyclist, and is likely to have at least one bike already, whether a mountain bike or a road machine, tourer, racer, or some combination of these. To such a rider, the ultimate satisfaction is owning a machine totally adapted to the purpose to which it will be put. The bike

Out-and-out racing machines

may never travel on the road, being transported to competitions on the roof of a car, or in a support vehicle of some kind. It is almost irrelevant to talk price. Mountain bikes of this class can be anything from £700 to £1,400. They will be designed around the individual rider, and crafted by skilled builders who are well able to match the idiosyncrasies of the rider with their own engineering skills, to produce the two-wheeled equivalent of a Stradivarius!

Naturally, bikes of this kind are pure race and trial machines. Weight will be down to the 26 lb mark; geometry can be anything the rider desires. The design of the frame will be more radical than the conventional diamond, down-sloping top tubes and very short chainstays, with the use of fairly exotic frame materials becoming more common. Shimano Deore XT component sets seem fairly standard, but custom-made parts such as brake levers, stems and seat pins are much in evidence.

For someone to own a bike of this sort, mountain biking must be more than a mere pastime, it has to be an obsession; the rider wants the satisfaction of knowing that the bike is a totally unique item.

The more you intend to spend on a bike, the more of your time you need to put into its design and selection. Like a good suit of clothes, it is being built for you alone, and no two people are exactly the same. At the other end of the scale, you also have to be careful, to make sure that you don't fall into the old trap of helping the dealers dispose of stock they couldn't sell to anyone else.

Whichever of the buyer profiles you

Good top-tube clearance

currently fall into, you will not be spending much less than £300, and that is enough money to deserve a little research. If you are just starting out, try to curb your impatience long enough to read a few books and magazines. Then you will be able to decide what general category of machine and which features appeal most to you and cater best for your needs. This book is designed to help with those choices, and to explain the terminology, so you feel less bewildered when listening to the dealer's sales patter.

A good cycle dealer will recognize the novice's confusion, and not try to pressure him or her into a hasty purchase. Indeed, with an eye to the future, the dealer may offer trial rides on a couple of machines, and some will switch components to suit, even with the relatively cheaper ranges of mountain bike. If a dealer resents you 'going away to think about it', do business with someone else. Getting a comfortable and safe bike – of any sort – is a more critical matter than even choosing a car. Cyclists are vulnerable creatures and are buying confidence as well as wheels. Bikes have less statutory and engineered protection than any car, and you should be able to trust and respect your dealer's judgement.

If you can, try to find a dealer who has some real experience of mountain bikes, rather than merely stocking a few models. Mountain bikes are different, and you need to know things that do not apply to conventional bikes – such as where you can legally ride off-road locally. If your dealer is unable to answer such a simple question, then it's most unlikely that the shop will be much use to you on other matters peculiar to the ATB.

Whatever you do, try to avoid buying your first mountain bike by mail order. All bicycles are highly tuned and adjusted machines, and this is particularly true for a device with eighteen gears, four cable-operated controls, fifteen ball races, and twenty or more points of regular adjustment. It is unreasonable to expect the novice to

▶ Buying second-hand ◀

1 With a friend holding the bike vertical, look along the wheels from the back and the front, to see they are in alignment. If they are even slightly out, accept no explanations, and walk away from the deal.

2 Spin the wheels while holding front and then rear wheels off the ground and, using the fork edge as a sight-line with the rim, look for a 'set' or irregularity in the wheel.

3 Listen to the bearings as the wheel spins. Make sure the valve comes to rest at the bottom, after a long, smooth spin. Check the brakes are not binding; if they are, move them out of contact with the rim by hand.

4 Examine the brake blocks for even wear. If a new set is fitted, look at the tyre walls for signs of damage caused by misaligned blocks. Look down on the blocks – they should 'toe in' slightly.

5 Holding the front brake on, push the bike forwards. If there is rocking movement, suspect the brake calliper fixing and ask for it to be tightened. If the rocking still occurs, the brakes are worn on their boss, the headset is worn, or both. Go home.

undo the case, straighten the bars, climb aboard and have a perfectly serviceable machine.

Any dealer worth the hire will either

6 Spin the pedals. They should be fairly quiet and revolve easily, but there must be no play if you pull and push them out from the spindle. Toe clips unbalance pedals and make their performance harder to judge.

7 Check the bottom-bracket for play by pulling and pushing the end of the crank. There should be no movement at all.

8 Examine the tyres. Wear should be even. Uneven does not necessarily mean mechanical malfunction, but it can mean the currrent owner is a lunatic, and the bike has been 'thrashed'.

9 Look carefully at all frame joints for signs of cracked paint or damaged welds. The most likely area for such damage will be the underneath of the junction between head and down tube. The slightest suspicion of damage here could mean a new frame.

10 Ride the bike. A serious and genuine seller will want you to ride it some distance, but you don't know each other, so offer to leave some valuable security for the machine (like half the asking price). But carry out tests 1–9 first – if the bike's a dog, the owner may feel happy to settle for half the price!

perform a pre-sale service personally, or have trained staff to do it. The machine will bed-in in the first 200 miles or so, and needs to be returned for running adjustments at around this time.

Perhaps worse than mail order, where at least you have some measure of protection under the Trading Standards Act, is buying second-hand machinery via an ad in a paper or magazine. If you must buy your first mountain bike second-hand, at least buy locally from someone you can ask detailed questions, and take a knowledgeable friend with you to check out the bike.

If that proves impossible, then at least carry out the ten checks shown on the left.

The ten tests will not in themselves guarantee satisfaction. Most of the things that go wrong in mountain bikes are matters of fine adjustment or wear in ancillary components, such as derailleurs, whereas these are tests for fundamental faults. But when buying second-hand you are by definition buying someone else's trouble as well as their joy, and you should allow enough in your budget for replacing those parts which have passed their useful lifetime. One-third of the saving over the new bike might be a useful sum to keep in mind.

If you are lucky enough to be buying a bespoke machine from a specialist builder, none of the above problems should worry you. But the process does have its own peculiarities. Frame builders are a fairly individual (some might say opinionated) bunch. They will have their way of doing things, and if you don't like it, you would do well to find someone more amenable to your ideas before a deal is struck. Most of the time, the frame builder will be right, and you should really listen if they question the angles you want set up or the bits you require brazed on. By all means discuss the frame, long and hard – that is part of the joy of the relationship, and certainly the price you will pay allows you advice and guidance. In the end, you should expect to get a good fusion of your ideas and the frame builder's skills and experience. If you're not happy, go elsewhere.

The mountain bike is an amalgam of parts, some specifically designed for it, some adapted from other types of cycle. This should not be taken to mean that it is not a highly developed and specialized machine. The field-testing of mountain bike components exceeds by far the stress that most riders will impose on their gear. The resulting products are, more often than not, excellent, and manufacturers are finding they can apply lessons learned from mountain bikes to other machines in their range.

All components will be highly stressed by off-road use, and no part of the machine can be a compromise on quality. It should also be remembered that mountain biking is an adventure sport, and riders are often taking quite

high levels of risk. In such circumstances, equipment failure is more than just inconvenient and irritating; it could be life-threatening. For this reason the manufacturers, from frame or component specialists through to the major companies assembling and selling complete ranges of bikes, have an obligation to see that all products are of high specification. This frequently means high cost.

There is an obligation too, on the user, to ensure that he or she does not unnecessarily risk life and limb by buying inadequate or unsuitable machines and equipment, or by failing to maintain the bike effectively in use. This section examines every component of the mountain bike in detail, to help create an understanding of the machine and its running equipment, so that potential mountain bikers can find their way through the jargon and mystique which inevitably surround a new and fashionable sport. Established riders, too, may find some fascination in the mixture of high-technology, traditional skills and inspired engineering design which has led to today's mountain bikes.

▶ FRAMES ◀

The frame on any type of bicycle performs a number of functions. It supports the body in a position where the rider can control the machine, convert the body's work into forward motion efficiently, and see where the bike is going. It provides the mounting-points for all the component parts of the machine – wheels, transmission, steering, braking and seating, lights and luggage platforms (if fitted). Finally, and depending on its design, it absorbs – together with the tyres – much of the 'shock' transmitted by the terrain over which the bicycle is passing.

Frame design is an almost infinitely variable affair. Bicycles, tricycles and tandems can be designed to perform a wide variety of work, on land, on water, and latterly, in flight. The basic design of this structure and mechanism, which harnesses the reciprocating energy of human legs, and uses it to produce motion, has been described as 'man's most beautiful machine'. It is certainly the most cost-effective, environmentally sensitive, healthy, pleasurable and – were it not for motor vehicles – one of the safest devices ever invented. The mountain bike, with its extremely versatile and rugged gearing, amazing strength/weight ratio and great adhesion and control, is probably the most efficient cycle yet designed.

The frame of a vehicle called on to perform so well under such adverse conditions has to be something special.

On the designers' 'shopping list' will be the following features:

- *stiffness* – to withstand the twisting and buckling forces induced by hard pedalling in low gears
- *lightness combined with strength* – to make the task of climbing easier
- *shock absorbency* – to minimize shock damage from fast progress over rough terrain
- *heat resistance* – to permit strong, safe metal-to-metal joints by brazing or welding
- *resilience* – to withstand reasonable impacts.

Such a range of properties – some apparently contradictory, such as stiffness and shock absorbency – is an essential attribute not only of the materials selected for the frame, but also of the manner in which it is constructed.

Next time you are in a cycle shop, compare the shape and style of a mountain bike with a road racer. You'll notice that the vertical tubes on the racer are more vertical than those on the mountain bike. This feature is not mere fashion. The more upright design gives faster, more 'lively' steering characteristics, and positions the rider almost directly over the pivot of the bottom-bracket of the cycle, permitting a stronger downward power stroke. However, far more road shock is transmitted upwards through the frame. Both these characteristics would be undesirable on a mountain bike, where generally slower, less 'twitchy' steering is a virtue, and smoothing out the shocks is vital. It is not only rider comfort that is at stake, but the very survival of the frame. Too upright and stiff a design for off-road use would mean undue stress on metal joints and eventual fatigue. Of course, not all the strain is borne by the frame; on mountain bikes, the tyres are a vital shock-absorbing medium, as well as being the means of gaining traction from the power transmitted. Careful attention to the geometry of the frame at design stage can nevertheless make for a more comfortable ride.

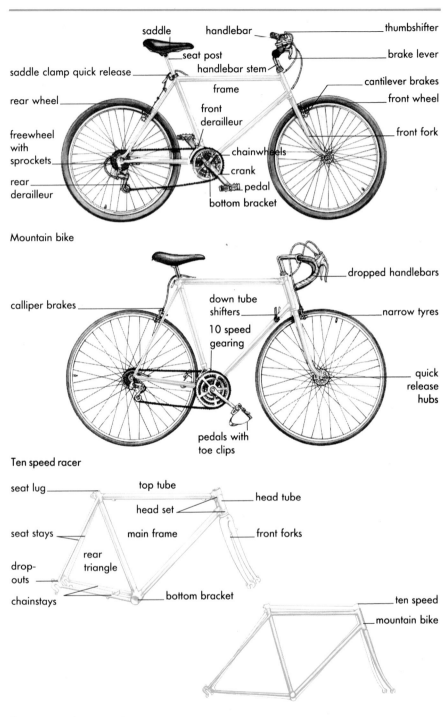

saddle

handlebar

thumbshifter

seat post

brake lever

handlebar stem

saddle clamp quick release

cantilever brakes

frame

rear wheel

front wheel

front
derailleur

freewheel
with
sprockets

front fork

chainwheels

crank

rear
derailleur

pedal

bottom bracket

Mountain bike

dropped handlebars

calliper brakes

down tube
shifters

narrow tyres

10 speed
gearing

quick
release
hubs

pedals with
toe clips

Ten speed racer

seat lug

top tube

head tube

head set

seat stays

main frame

front forks

drop-
outs

rear
triangle

chainstays

bottom bracket

ten speed

mountain bike

Frame geometry comparison

▶ Geometry ◀

So what is this 'geometry', and what variations exist within the category of machine we are examing?

To understand the subject fully, we must first know the main parts of the conventional triangulated or diamond frame, and understand their function. There are two vertical slanting main tubes on a bike. One is at the front; it carries the stem for the handlebars, into which the front wheel forks and steering bearings are inserted. This is known as the head tube or steering tube. Roughly parallel to this is the seat tube, from the top of which projects the seat pin and saddle, and at the bottom of which is mounted the bottom-bracket, which holds the chainwheel spindle and bearings. The angles which these two tubes subtend to the vertical plane govern the 'geometry' of the bike. Also important is the 'rake' of the front forks, the height of the bottom-bracket, and the length of the chainstays, which, together with the seat stays, form the rear triangle which retains the back wheel. The structure is completed by the (usually) horizontal top tube, which connects the seat and head tubes at the top, and the down tube, which goes between the bottom-bracket and head tube.

Through the geometric construction the designer has to give the rider the ability to:

- produce the optimum climbing power
- maintain stability in fast, uneven descents
- have good ground clearance
- manœuvre around obstacles with precision
- change weight distribution to suit varying conditions.

You will see that the designer's job is no easy one; already conflicting requirements have crept into the specification. As we have seen from the racer, maximum power is produced by a more vertical seat tube, positioning the rider over the bottom-bracket. But this is at odds with the desire to help iron out the rough spots in the ride by producing a more laid-back, slanting seat and head tube. Precise steering is effected by an upright head tube, but stability downhill is better served by more slope in this angle.

The task is not wholly impossible. Some of the requirements are achieved in frame design, some by the way the front forks are curved or raked; clever design of seat fixings and handlebar stems marry the best all-round frame to the optimum rider position.

In general terms, mountain bikes have their head tubes at an angle of between 69° and 73°, giving less responsive or 'quick' steering than, say a racing bike with a head angle of some 74°, but enhancing greatly the comfort and predictability which make for good handling at speed on rough surfaces, and the ability to 'forgive' minor steering errors. This will be married with a longish fork 'rake' or curved section, which improves the handling still further on uneven ground.

Many mountain bikes – particularly those 'first generation' machines deriving from the early experiments in California, repeat the 69° angle for the seat tube, giving a parallel diamond section to the frame. However, this tends to require the rear chainstays to be elongated to give sufficient clearance between the back wheel and the seat tube. This means that a long wheelbase is produced, which is both stable and comfortable downhill on rough going, but loses some hill-climbing efficiency, because the rider is neither positioned over the bottom-bracket (to achieve the optimum power stroke) nor with all weight over the rear wheel (to aid traction). In practice, the problems tend to be eased both by the very low-ratio gearing available to the rider and by the fact that most mountain bikers rapidly develop a very mobile technique, shifting their weight to suit terrain and gradient. Such parallel geometry produces a fairly 'gentle' bike, well-suited to the novice because of its predictable nature in fast descents.

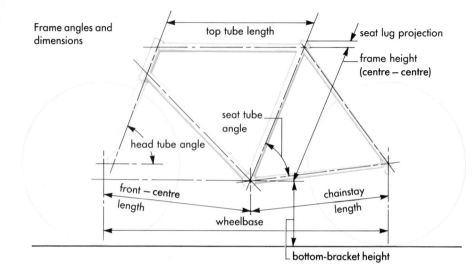

Frame angles and dimensions

top tube length

seat lug projection

frame height (centre – centre)

seat tube angle

head tube angle

front – centre length

chainstay length

wheelbase

bottom-bracket height

Frame design has moved on to a second and even third generation of bikes, with shorter wheelbases and other subtle changes to the bike's geometry designed to confer various handling virtues. Most popular frames have retained the shallower head tube angles, while tending towards steeper (around 72°/73°) seat tubes; some custom-made racing machines have also adopted this angle for the head tube, giving faster steering, but requiring a more experienced rider. But for general riding, on- and off-road, a laid-back long-wheelbase frame, with a relatively high bottom-bracket to give good clearance for pedals and chainset, will cope admirably with all but the most exacting competition riding.

Of course, the diamond frame pattern is not the only genuine mountain bike design, although it is the most popular, and forms the basis of most variants. More recognizable derivatives slope the top tube downwards towards the seat tube, in order to give more clearance between crotch and frame and a smaller, stiffer assembly. In another offshoot, the head tube almost vanishes entirely, as the top and down tubes meet each other in an effort to reduce frame size. This makes for greater

stiffness and less weight, both desirable features; the frame can be made to fit normal-sized riders by a longer than usual handlebar stem and seat pin. It has been mentioned elsewhere that mountain bike frames should be at least 2 to 2.5 inches smaller than the frame which would suit the same rider on a normal bicycle.

▶ Frame materials ◀

The most popular material for frames is seamless alloy-steel tubing. Much research has gone into producing exactly the right blends of steel with chromium, manganese tungsten and other materials, to suit the exacting needs of a high-performance bicycle. Recently, the more specialized manufacturers have produced types of tubing designed specifically for mountain bikes – examples include Tange Prestige MTB, Tange MTB, Ishiwata MTB D and Reynolds 531 ATB – and other manufacturers will doubtless follow suit. The advantage is in having thicker walls and outside diameters, which can meet the stresses of off-road work. The increased weight of such up-rated tubing is alleviated by 'butting', which means the tubes are manufactured with thicker ends than middles. This provides strength where it is needed, to cope with the heat of the joining process and the stresses of ground shock and torsion on joints.

It is important to ensure that a frame is built of the 'branded' steel, or combination of steels selected, throughout. You can often check this by looking for the transfer on the bike which identifies the material used. For the enthusiast who wishes to know more about the theory and manufacturing detail of frame tubing, *The Mountainbike Book* by Rob Van Der Plas is an excellent reference (see Bibliography). However, a word of warning – metallurgy is a highly specialized subject, not to be mastered by casual reading. It is wiser to be advised by experts on the materials used in your new frame, than to try to specify them yourself on the basis of a little reading. By and large, the manufacturers provide an excellent product, and there is little to be gained by using inferior materials to cut costs.

Of course, steel is not the only material used in frame construction. Aluminium has its place, used either in combination with steel or on its own. The arguments for and against aluminium in mountain bikes are complex.

The material is certainly lighter than alloy steel, and lightness is a goal in itself, since a less heavy machine rides the bumps more easily, attracts less impact shock, and so requires less absolute strength. In theory, this should tip the scales substantially in favour of aluminium; it is one-third the weight of steel and has much better vibration-damping characteristics. But it's considerably weaker than steel, and is less easy to join. Together these two characteristics mean that, frame for frame, the aluminium version will have significantly thicker dimensions and need more substantial engineering to achieve the same strength. This tends to eliminate the weight advantage almost entirely.

Some builders have opted for a mix, in order to blend the favourable characteristics of both. Aluminium tubing in steel lugs; aluminium forming the main 'diamond' of head, top, seat and down tubes, with steel in the rear triangle and front forks, is one formula which delivers benefits. Another exotic but promising mixture encases thin-walled aluminium tubing in super-strong Kevlar, bonded into alloy lug castings. Such space-age confections are expensive

now but, if they prove successful, their price will be drastically reduced by the economics of mass-production.

For the time being, aluminium is the alternative to steel with the greatest market availability, and two manufacturers – Cannondale and Muddy Fox – offer reasonably priced, well-tested versions. If you just must have that space-age technology, Reflex of America have started exporting their aluminium/carbon-fibre/Kevlar hybrid to Europe in a limited edition.

High-quality alloy steel, used in butted, oversize 'ATB' gauge, still remains the most popular, economic and efficient material in which to build mountain bikes, and is likely to remain so for some years to come.

▶ Joining and bonding ◀

The joints between the various frame tubes are obviously critical. It is here that the stresses and shocks impact most strongly, and the junctions must be capable of withstanding them. A frame breakage during a descent is more than just expensive – it might be terminal!

In the early days of mountain bike development, all frames had to be welded or brazed, since lugs were not available in the appropriate sizes. Such frames have more than proved their durability, and although lugged frames are now available – and very elegant they look – straight tube-to-tube welding and brazing, performed skilfully, is a perfectly sound means of frame construction.

Brazing and welding are two joining methods which look the same, but are in fact quite different. Welding is a method which heats the metal surfaces to be joined to their melting points, and then fuses them together. Brazing employs less heat, using a brazing rod of metal of a lower melting-point, which is run into the joint and acts as a strong bond. Brazing is used either to form straight tube-to-tube connections, or in conjunction with lugs. Welding is suitable both for steel and aluminium,

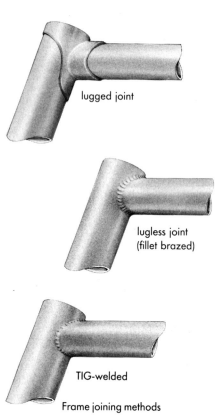

lugged joint

lugless joint
(fillet brazed)

TIG-welded

Frame joining methods

but requires rather thicker walls than brazing, to avoid heat damage. It is carried out in an inert gas atmosphere to prevent corrosion, hence the terms 'TIG' or 'WIG' welded: tungsten or wolfram inert gas. By far the majority of mountain bike frames are TIG welded; some show fairly obvious evidence of the fusion of the tubing, others are treated cosmetically to make the joints smoother. In either case, the method is satisfactory when performed by a competent manufacturer or frame builder.

Joining aluminium and the more unusual building materials is less straightforward. As we have seen, aluminium can be welded, but this

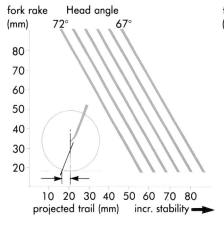

fork rake (mm)

Head angle 72° 67°

80
70
60
50
40
30
20

10 20 30 40 50 60 70 80
projected trail (mm)   incr. stability ➤

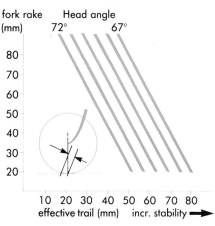

fork rake (mm)

Head angle 72° 67°

80
70
60
50
40
30
20

10 20 30 40 50 60 70 80
effective trail (mm)   incr. stability ➤

Unicrown fork

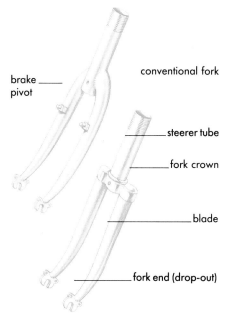

brake pivot

conventional fork

steerer tube

fork crown

blade

fork end (drop-out)

takes more skill than with high-alloy steels, and is therefore less amenable to low-cost mass-production techniques. Aluminium welded frames are employed by a number of manufacturers, while others are experimenting with alternative forms of bonding, including epoxy adhesives of great strength (and expense), usually in conjunction with steel or cast alloy lugs to give added stiffness and support to the joint.

▶ Forks and bearings ◀

Strictly speaking, the front forks are an integral part of the frame, although some builders allow a modicum of choice in the type of fork construction. The most popular type of fork for mountain bikes is the 'unicrown' pattern, where the fork blades curve into a welded or brazed join with the steering post which fits into the head tube, resting on a bearing at each end. This derives from the BMX and is a very strong and stylish fork. Other types use lugs and reinforcing castings of different types, and selection (where options are available) is very much a matter of personal choice.

The bottom-bracket is at the core of a frame, for it is here that the greatest number of frame tubes meet, and this is also where the spindle which carries the chainset – the converter of human strength into mechanical power – is housed in its bearings. Pattern of bottom-bracket will be dependent on the type of frame joining used (lugged or lugless), on the width of spindle, allowing up to three chainwheels to be fitted, and on whether the down tube is flattened to give enhanced lateral resistance and increased wheel clearance.

▶ Frame fittings ◀

At one time, specialized high-performance bicycles had the minimum of brazed-on bits, to make them more adaptable to different components, and to reduce all-up weight. Today the opposite is true, with a plethora of bosses, screw threads, appendages and locating-points to make positioning of ancillary equipment permanent, and prevent the inevitable stressing of clips which can lead to 'iffy' gear changing, floppy control cables, lost pumps and bottles, and a host of other undesirable ailments.

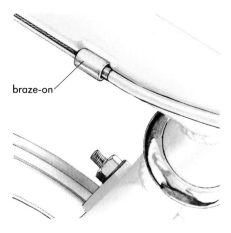

braze-on

Drop-outs

Let's start with the most vital frame component next to the tubing itself: the 'drop-outs'. These are the plates at the end of the front and rear fork assembly, used to secure the wheels to the frame. At one time, cheaper bicycles employed slotted plates, welded or brazed into the fork ends, to perform this function. Now, far greater strength and precision are required, and drop-outs fabricated from wide-gauge cast steel or aluminium are used, designed to ensure that the wheel is positively located in one position only – obviously an advantage from the point of view of derailleur and brake operation.

braze-on

Of course, such an arrangement can mean that a frame is dedicated to one manufacturer's brake or derailleur assembly, but this is in keeping with the 'designed from the ground up' trend for modern ATBs. In fact, the major gear-mechanism manufacturers supply frame makers with their own drop-outs to ensure optimum performance.

Brake bosses

Brake bosses are probably the next most vital 'bit' to be attached to the frame, and the normal arrangement is to have tandem-type cantilevers attached to the front forks, and either the same arrangement on the rear seat stays, or a 'U-brake' assembly on the seat stay, or

braze-on

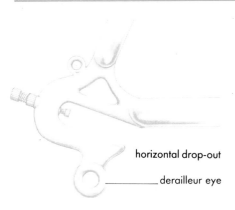

horizontal drop-out

_____ derailleur eye

Drop-outs

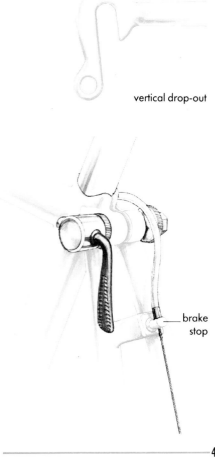

vertical drop-out

brake stop

underneath the chainstay. The recent fashion for this latter form of attachment has not been without controversy. The 'beneath the chainstay' position does seem to place the brake neatly in the path of a great deal of dust, grit, mud and wet, none of which are particular allies of brake performance. The manufacturers claim that this position offers a 'clean look' to the frame. Perhaps, but a clean brake in an accessible place would be preferable. It is to be hoped that this piece of fashionable nonsense will soon disappear from the catalogues.

Cantilever brakes

Cantilever brakes, in addition to bosses, need a positive stop for the outer casing of the brake cables, to allow the inner cable to be retracted inside its casing, thus exerting the operating pull on the cantilever mechanism. This can take the form of a bridge between the seat stays, and is usually used in conjunction with brazed-on cable guides for the brake and gear-control cables. The front and rear derailleur control cables are often bared from the point where they first connect with the frame to shortly before where they reach the mechanisms. The bare cable is transported around the bottom-bracket by means of pulleys or channels – a significant saving of weight over a fully cased cable.

Other brazed-on bits may include a peg on the right rear seat stay for hanging the chain when removing a wheel; pegs for a pump; and threaded fittings to enable the easy installation of mudguards, panniers, bottles and so on. These can be mounted in a variety of positions; most favoured places are the drop-outs for the mudguards and panniers, seat and down tube for bottles.

If you are fortunate enough to be specifying your own frame, you can decide how many bits you want added, and where to put them, but it is obvious from the very full specifications in manufacturers' catalogues that they have researched consumer taste in this area fairly well.

▶ POINTS OF CONTACT ◀

The frame, as well as contributing much to the ride, supports all the component parts of the bike, locating them in the correct position for rider comfort and convenience, and ensuring their complete immobility in use. Of these various components, those with which the rider comes into physical contact are of paramount importance, for no mountain bike will do its job successfully if the rider is not comfortable. The seating arrangements are the highest priority, since the saddle and its ancillaries support the greater part of the rider's weight, more so than with dropped-handlebar machines.

▶ Seat pins ◀

The seat pin is the tube which is inserted into the seat tube of the frame, fitting snugly to the inside diameter and carrying at its top end a device for attaching and adjusting the saddle. It is secured in the frame by a 'binder bolt' assembly. On a mountain bike, these components are crucial; indeed, they were the subject of some of the first engineering development work, which gave the machine its great versatility and set the pattern for today's models.

The Californian ace Garry Fisher was the first to realize the importance of rapid saddle-height adjustment on a mountain bike. A low seating position improves stability and control when descending, a higher seat gives greater power when climbing. Spanners in pockets are not just uncomfortable – in a fall they can become painfully lodged in bits of the anatomy, so some alternative means of adjusting the seat was required. The answer came in the kind of quick-release lever mechanism used to secure the wheels of road-racing bikes. This was adapted to replace the binder bolt at the top of the seat tube and the problem of quick and safe seat adjustment was solved.

The seat pin itself has undergone a process of evolution from the chromium-plated steel extrusions standard on the old Schwinn 'clunkers'. As the mountain bike developed, so it became accepted that a smaller frame than was standard for road use had great advantages. It was lighter and stiffer, and took the top tube further

tubular   bottom-adjusting

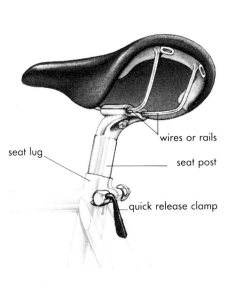

wires or rails

seat lug

seat post

quick release clamp

More would-be cyclists have decided to pursue some other sport as a result of a badly chosen, maladjusted or just plain lousy saddle, than from any other cause. Hardly surprising, since the male and female anatomies are most vulnerable in the pelvic regions, for reasons beyond the scope of this book but fairly familiar to us all.

If the above statement is true for road bikes, it is doubly so for mountain bikes, where you can add constant vibration and pounding, chafing, bruising and unpleasant overheating to the repertoire of masochism suffered by those who pay insufficient attention to their seating arrangements. If you believe it is macho to use one of those thinly disguised razor blades upon which the shaven-limbed, skin-tight-Lycra-clad road racers perch, when you're on a machine for descending rock-strewn high passes, your leisure hours might be more richly rewarded in self-flagellation or polar skin-diving.

From the foregoing, you might deduce that the subject of saddles is regarded as important by the writer. True. Not only comfort, but health is involved. That most delicate area of male and female anatomy may, on some of us at least, appear well-padded, but in truth it consists of a pelvic arch made of bone, inside which all kinds of complicated soft bits are accommodated, bits which – in either male or female form – do not appreciate hard, unrelieved pummelling over long periods of time. The bones of the pelvic arch and posterior need to be well supported on a firm base. The saddle has to provide that firm base. It must be constructed in a way which avoids chafing the inside upper thighs, and be made of materials which will mould to the individual body contours, and breathe to avoid causing excessive sweating.

Such a spec is a tall order. Add to it the requirement that a mountain bike saddle will also be rather more yielding than that fitted to a road bike, in order

away from the rider in the event of a crash. However, the saddle and handlebars had to be extended much more than on a road bike. It was also necessary to have a much more accurate and firm way of selecting and securing saddle adjustment. The saddle takes much more of the rider's weight, over much rougher surfaces than other bikes. Therefore, seat height and angle need to be capable of both fine adjustment and absolute fixing.

Once again, the road bike provided the answer, and the sophisticated alloy seat pins of the road racer, with their micro-adjusting clamps – easily accessible to an Allen key, but totally secure in use – were the answer. To overcome the small-frame problem, the seat pins were made much longer, so that even at extreme saddle heights a safe margin of seat pin remained within the seat tube of the bike. A number of manufacturers now offer ATB and mountain bike seat pins, either as individual items or within a 'group' of components such as stems, brakes, chainwheels and derailleurs.

not to unseat the rider on the nearest tree root or half-buried rock, and you have yet another design problem for the bike builder. The problem, if not solved, has been eased considerably in recent years. The search for the perfect bike saddle is probably eternal, but a number of patterns and manufacturers have come quite close. Two schools of thought prevail: **sprung** and **anatomical**.

sprung leather saddle

Sprung saddles

In the sprung saddles, the famous old name of Brooks, almost as old as the bicycle itself, is the doyen. What Brooks don't know about making leather bicycle saddles would probably cripple you anyway! For mountain bikes, the B66 Champion is as good as they come, and although – in common with all leather saddles – it will require a period of running-in, it will eventually conform to your vital statistics like a second skin. Mind you, if someone else borrows your bike, it will probably do them no good at all, but that can be an argument in favour!

Like all organic materials, leather needs looking after, and later pages are devoted to maintenance, but such a component is a lifetime investment, and deserves a little coddling. Leather scores highly against other points of the specification too. It doesn't induce sweating as much as other materials, and a specialist bike shop will 'butcher' the frame to avoid chafing your thighs, and fit oversize rivets to withstand the strain of adjustment. If you *are* having surgery performed on your saddle, make sure it is done by a mountain bike expert; saddles altered to make them more suitable for road racing are not improved for mountain biking!

Anatomical saddles

The leather saddle with springs relies on the ability of leather to mould to the rider's dimensions to provide firm location and the springs to give suspension. The second style of saddle,

unsprung nylon saddle

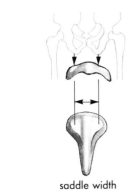

saddle width

anatomical, is a different formula, developed recently using technology borrowed from the biomedical industry, and put to great effect in making the flexible, foot-hugging interiors of ski boots.

The concept is fairly simple – a silicone-based rubber-like material with the property of 'memory'. It holds an impression of a shape pressed into it, is placed on exactly the right parts of a base, and anatomically designed to support the pelvic structure. The saddle is grooved down its centre to prevent nerve pinching – which can cause numbness of the crotch for men and painful soreness for women – and the whole is covered with hide and mounted on a light saddle frame. The theory is that such a seat will be rapidly 'broken in' to the rider, not just once, but every time he or she rides the bike for any distance, and so accommodate the bottoms of more than one rider. The hide covering imparts all the virtues of leather, and the silicon layers have great properties of shock absorbency.

The theory works. The writer has such a saddle on his mountain bike, and it was broken-in within a week, yet pronounced comfortable by a mountain-biking nephew who borrowed the bike to break a few local rocks recently. Madison are among the leaders in this field, and have a wide range of designs, including several specifically developed for mountain bikes. The anatomical approach has enabled really sensible and properly constructed versions for women too, instead of merely broadened versions of the instruments of torture available for men.

▶ BARS, STEMS AND GRIPS ◀

Although flat, wide handlebars characterize the ATB, some very experienced manufacturers of respected machinery (Muddy Fox and Bridgestone) offer top-of-the range models with dropped bars. This is probably to cater for the cyclo-cross devotees who are realizing the limitations of their rather frail cross-country machines, and seeking a compromise with purism. Dropped bars are the exception rather than the rule, and the classic mountain bike will sport flat, slightly curved (rather than straight) bars of around 26 inches or less in width. These will be manufactured in aluminium or alloy steel (often just as light) and mounted in an upward-facing stem, sometimes aluminium but more often steel, secured at the bars by two binder bolts, and in the head tube of the bike by an expander bolt. Both of these fixings will, on higher class machinery, employ recessed bolts designed to be opened by an Allen key; the stem, as well as supporting the handlebars, will often

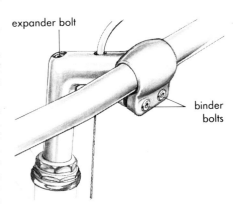

provide part of the channel for the front brake cable.

The bars too are multi-purpose. They play a major role in rider support, especially when you stand on the pedals; together with lean applied from the buttocks and shoulders, they are involved in the complex business of steering and weaving the bike round obstacles. The braking and gear-changing mechanisms are located on the bars, and they often provide the mounting for lights and luggage. If the mountain bike were a ship, the bars would most certainly be the bridge.

Shape of bars and the layout of the controls on them have a limited amount of flexibility to suit personal choice, and there are no hard and fast rules. The best result is usually arrived at over time, when the pattern of individual usage emerges and adjustments can be made to suit. You will find that for city work narrower bars are preferable, allowing you to squirm through narrow gaps; off-road, a little more leverage can be an advantage, but the 26-inch maximum width limit is pretty much the widest any rider will need, and many will prefer less.

As to steel or aluminium, the weight difference is hardly significant. For bars, the high-alloy steels in the gauges suitable for mountain biking – and with the lengths of tubing involved – are almost the same weight as the equivalent strength of aluminium. However, for stems, steel is definitely preferable for serious off-road work. Aluminium may be OK, but imagination is a powerful thing, and a breakage in this area on a swift downhill slalom is not an attractive thought. If your machine is mainly for touring, with some gentle off-road work of a non-competitive nature, then the weight advantage of an all-aluminium set might shave off a few valuable ounces. If you intend to race boulders down landslides, make a small concession to sanity and settle for steel.

The stem, as we saw earlier, plays a part in the braking process by acting as both a guide and a stop for the outer casing of the front cantilever cable. This adds yet more importance to a component which is involved in steering, climbing and balancing, as well as – when the right stem is fitted – contributing much to rider comfort. It is by no means guaranteed that the item which comes with your shiny new machine will be ideally suited to your physique, or to the use you intend to make of your mount. Choosing the right stem is covered on pages 73–4, and is almost as important a decision as the saddle, for at no time are you out of contact with this component (as long as things are going right!).

Grips are the most intimate part of the bar and stem arrangement, for it is to these humble objects that we cling with a prayer on our lips and blue sky beneath both wheels. It's surprising what a difference the right grip can make, and in my opinion the only formula to have 'got it right' for mountain bikes so far is the closed-cell foam variety. It is no coincidence that 'Grab-On' grips are fitted on most top-of-the-range bikes, and it is the best-value-for-money 'mod' to any machine without them.

Grips have to stay grippable when sweaty and wet, absorb shocks and vibrations, be warm in the cold and cool in the hot (sounds like a commercial for the ideal lover) and, finally, must not move, under any circumstances. Grab-Ons are comparatively expensive, but worth every penny.

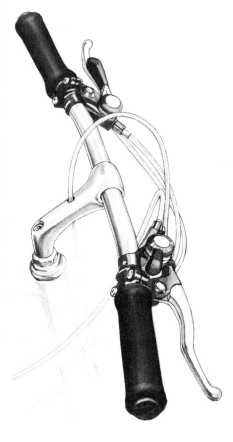

Bars and controls

▶ PEDALS ◀

Pedals are one of those components that either get insufficient thought, or are the subject of economies when people build a bike to a price. This is a pity, for, like all the other parts with which the rider makes regular contact, they have an effect on comfort, efficiency and enjoyment out of all proportion to their cost. It should also be remembered that the pedals are the first link in the chain of power transfer from you to the bike's transmission.

When you select pedals for a mountain bike, three questions are important.

1. Is the machine primarily for touring/commuting, with some off-road fun at weekends?

2. If you are building/buying a racer, what kind of competition will you be specializing in: hill climb, observed trials or cross-country racing?

3. What sort of clothing will you be primarily wearing when riding?

For mixed touring, commuting and off-road fun, a sturdy pair of 'bear trap' type pedals, aluminium centres, sealed bearings and steel serrated rims can't be beaten. They should be fitted without toe-clips, and reflectors for night-time road work are sensible. Choose a good make. (Shimano or HTI are fine, at opposite ends of the price scale, and most ready-assembled ATBs of a mid-to-upper price bracket come fitted with good pedals of this type.) The absence of toe clips will have a negligible effect on performance at this level, and will enable you to part company with your bike that much quicker. This type of pedal relies on grip between the shoe and the serrated cage to transfer power efficiently, so some attention to shoe sole tread is necessary. Most trainers with good deeply treaded soles will do, and if you are on the sort of terms with your bank to run to the expense of some of the imported shoes for mountain bikers, you will most certainly outpose the opposition on the morning run to the station!

If competition is in prospect, then a different view should be taken of toe clips. There is no doubt that, for many branches of the sport, toe clips add power and control, and some events, such as hill-climb, cannot be attempted without them. It is still debatable whether they are strictly necessary for observed trials or downhill slalom; if in doubt, try both ways and see what gives the greatest feeling of security.

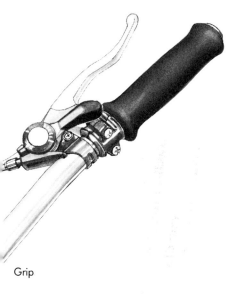

Grip

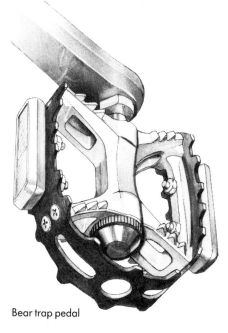

Bear trap pedal

If you *are* fitting clips, then there are a number of styles and patterns to choose from, and materials can be both steel and tough plastic. The latter certainly has virtues; it doesn't break as easily when crushed and is cheaper – and mountain bikes can be tough on toe clips. However, you should not economize on the straps, which need to be of a durable hard leather with really good and effective quick-release straps. To skimp here is senseless.

Clips cannot be fitted to the plastic-caged pedals which are on some of the cheaper mountain bikes; these should not be used for serious off-road use. The metal bear-trap variety is still the best all-round choice; Suntour supply a pedal specifically designed for fitting toe clips.

A final point on clothing – if your mountain bike is to be your only form of transport, remember that pedals are bad for ordinary shoes. Try to wear trainers only on the bike or, if you must wear good leather-soled shoes, have rubber soles attached, and change them regularly.

▶ WHEELS ◀

The wheel is one of the most abused parts of the mountain bike, expected to carry bike and rider across rock and gravel, down city steps, through glutinous mud and snow. To endure such punishment, the wheel must be strong, light and corrosion-free.

No mountain bike deserving the name will be equipped with steel-rimmed wheels. The weight penalty is too high, especially since revolving weight increases with speed. Additionally, the braking characteristics of chromium-plated steel rims can't compare with hard-anodized aluminium, and steel rusts.

The standard mountain bike wheels are 26 inches in diameter, and the inside rim width is just under the inch (around 20 mm), although this varies between makes, with little apparent effect on tyre fit or adhesion. Good makes of rim are fitted with ferrules through which the spoke tensioners pass, so that tightening the spokes does not damage the rim surface.

As in all things, fashions change. **Rims** are presently tending to become narrower and more oval in section, and black hard-anodizing is 'in'. This is held to improve the braking characteristics of the wheel. Manufacturers to look for in rims include Mavic and Ascenti, while Araya of Japan produce a good lower-cost rim which makes a very strong wheel and is fitted to many stock bikes.

Spokes come in single-gauge or double-butted varieties, and only stainless steel is worth considering for mountain bikes. Most wheel builders build ATB wheels in single-gauge stainless steel, and this has the advantage that a wheel with such spokes, while heavier, stays true longer with a spoke missing. Mountain bikes are more prone to spoke breakage than other machines, owing both to the rugged nature of the surfaces covered, and also to the undergrowth and other bits of the environment which are more likely to intrude into the spoked part of the wheels as they pass. It is a good idea to become familiar with replacing broken spokes, and carry a spare or two and the requisite tool.

Hubs are hard-working machines, being the means of attachment of the wheels to the bicycle frame, via either a solid spindle secured by wheel nuts, or hollow spindles containing quick-release mechanisms. The hub supports the wheel, providing the central location point for the spokes, and it carries within it the bearing upon which the wheel revolves. In the case of the rear hub, it also carries the cluster or block of geared sprockets which form the 'gearbox' of the bike.

Hubs are nearly always of light alloy construction, can be large- or small-flanged, and provide varying degrees of protection from water and dust for their bearings. This is important, since any running resistance at the hub has a serious effect on overall performance, but is also an indication that bearing life

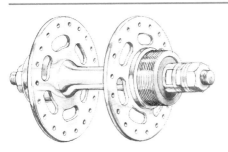

large-flange hub

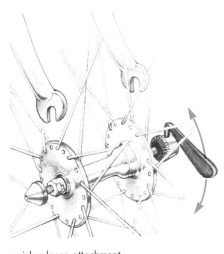

quick release attachment

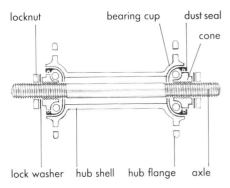

locknut   bearing cup   dust seal

                                    cone

lock washer   hub shell   hub flange   axle

hub cross-section

is limited. Wheels should rotate noiselessly until the valve stem of the tyre is at the lowest point, when the wheel is held clear of the ground. If they don't, and the brakes are not binding, suspect the bearings.

There is no fixed opinion about the 'right' hub for mountain bikes. Both wide- and narrow-flanged hubs are fitted, and there is a theory that, while the wide-flanged variety may make a stronger wheel (because the spokes are shorter and the longer perimeter of the hub can accommodate more spokes), the effect is cancelled out by the steeper angle of the spoke heads in the flange, which encourages breakage. If the hub fitted or selected is a good make, of middle or high cost, then this is unlikely to be a problem. The use to which you are going to put the machine should govern your choice. Wheels which need to withstand the constant rigour of off-road riding will benefit from wide flanges and a higher spoke-count; urban and light touring ATBs will feel the weight advantage of smaller hubs and fewer spokes.

More significant is the protection granted to the bearings within the hubs. These need to be sealed against dust and wet to improve their running performance and life expectancy. Two types of bearing are common, and both are satisfactory within the context of a 'good' hub. **'Cartridge' bearings** are sealed for life, and certainly do a good job. However, like all of us, they have a certain life expectancy, and if they seize up off-road somewhere, it won't be practical to replace them on a wind-swept hillside. Of course, if you get into the habit of checking hub bearings regularly by performing the test mentioned above, spinning the wheel and listening to the bearing for signs of distress, then you are unlikely to be caught unawares.

Replaceable bearings can also be sealed against dust and moisture, and although they are not quite as secure as the cartridge variety, they do have the virtue of easy and cheap replacement. In fact, good preventive

QR hubs
(small flange)

maintenance will ensure as much reliability as the sealed-for-life variety, unless you intend to spend most of your time cycling down submerged river beds. Don't laugh, someone wither does it, or will shortly seek sponsorshop for it!)

The other major choice with hubs is **quick-release mechanisms** (QR) or **wheel nuts**. The chief advantage of QR is being able to remove the wheel quickly to deal with a puncture. In a road race, using light tubular tyres, a skilled rider can be back in contention very quickly. This is less likely off-road, where everything takes so much longer (beaded tyres, masses of mud, a puncture to mend rather than a roll-off, roll-on job), so the major speed advantage of a QR mechanism is lost. For the ATB, the main advantage of quick-

release is that you can remove the front wheel for transport or security reasons. This is why you will often see a QR mech only on the front wheel of mountain bikes, especially in towns. The greater security of nuts is preferred by many riders on the rear wheel – although with dedicated drop-outs, where only one position of wheel is possible, the quick-release is probably perfectly safe. If cost is the prime factor, a good pair of solid axle hubs is a wiser option than a mid-range quick-release ensemble.

Rear hubs are of necessity narrow, to permit the fitting of (in the main) six-sprocketed gear blocks for the rear derailleur. One expensive but very convenient variation to the standard threaded variety, produced by Shimano, replaces the thread for the block by a spline which allows rapid change of sprockets. This can be an advantage when you are competing in a mountain biking event with several disciplines – hill climb, observed trial, cross-country and downhill slalom – and the ability to vary the range of ratios available can be useful. But for the majority of riders, eighteen gears suffice.

There is an increasing trend towards wheels of unequal size on competition mountain bikes. The smaller (24-inch) rear wheel makes possible shorter chainstays, and therefore shorter wheelbases, thus aiding climbing ability. The smaller wheel also lowers the ratios of the gears fitted, and this too is a benefit on really steep climbs. However, such an extreme measure is out of place on a machine for mixed use, unless posing is high up on the priority list!

▶TYRES◀

Tyre width can vary from 1.5 inches to 2.25 inches on mountain bikes, depending on the predominant use of the machine. If you're planning a lot of road riding and the occasional off-road jaunt, a tyre of 1.5 inches, with a raised, smooth centre portion, surrounded by knobs to give traction in mud and other slippery surfaces, is the ideal. This generates far less rolling resistance in road riding, but still gives reasonable grip on bridleways and unsurfaced paths.

If you do an appreciable amount of your riding off-road, but still travel on tarmac to get to your routes, then something more substantial is required. Stick to a 1.5 or 1.9 inch tyre, but go for the off-road pattern tread, which is heavily studded all over, and will permit you to increase its traction by under-inflation.

Those fortunate enough to transport their mighty mountain muncher to the field of battle on the roof rack of a

support vehicle, and never let it near a surfaced road, will be able to enjoy the ultimate rough-stuff luxury of uncompromising 2.5 inch competition tyres. This much rubber has such grip that the tyres are positively uncomfortable to ride on the road, they are noisy and add drag. A bike thus equipped will be significantly slower on any smooth surface, but performance off-road is unbeatable, especially if the tyres are run 'soft'.

Mountain bike tyres are all of the 'beaded' variety. That is, they are covers which go over an inner tube, and two steel wires run round the lips of the covers to keep them seated in the rim. The tyres are used in conjunction with high-pressure inner tubes. The

The Shimano cassette system and rear QR

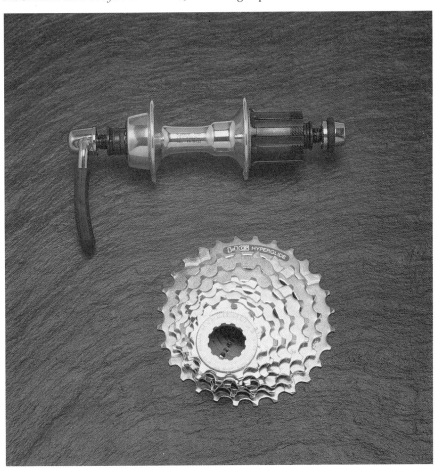

recommended pressures will be moulded on to the casing, and you will find your own preferred pressure with experiment. Remember, though, that although lower pressures give greater adhesion, punctures can be caused if the pressure is so low as to allow the inner tube to be pinched between the rim and a rock or tree root. It follows that you should leave enough air in to avoid this. There are those riders who, in an attempt to shed the last gram of weight, leave the pump at home. This is foolish on a mountain bike, and the pump should be regarded as a necessity rather than an accessory, with due regard paid to its fixing position on the frame. You may well need to use the pump at least once in a mixed road and rough terrain ride and, if you puncture, you are completely lost without it.

Tyre composition, construction and tread pattern forms a specialized subject in itself, and one that has gained new impetus from the arrival of the ATB. Development continues, but a wide range of tyre patterns exists at the time of writing, from a completely smooth 'slick' made by Nutrack for city bikes, to an almost agricultural patterned tyre by Specialized Ground Control, which looks as if it would climb walls. A broad selection of patterns are available in all widths, and some are now equipped with a Kevlar belt, inserted under the tread to add further protection against punctures.

All the major manufacturers of cycle tyres have patterns either specifically designed for ATBs or perfectly suitable for use on them, and tyre selection becomes a matter of matching riding requirements with available budget. Obviously, you get what you pay for, and it's unwise to economize on tyres, simply because they just don't last very long, especially if you use your bike to its limits. Recently, a number of the better names in mountain bikes have started to brand tyres – Ritchey and Muddy Fox for example – and these are worth considering alongside the offerings of the traditional manufacturers.

▶ TRANSMISSIONS ◀

The purpose of variable transmission systems, or gearing, in a cycle is to allow the rider to maintain a similar cadence (pedalling rate) over varying gradients. The transmission does this by changing the ratio of revolutions of the front chainwheel to the distance covered by the rear wheel. 'Low' gears require more revolutions than 'high' gears, and are therefore more suitable for climbing, since they reduce the amount of sheer physical strength required to propel the bike uphill.

It has not always been possible to 'gear' cycles. The earliest machines had the pedals directly attached to the front wheel spindle, so that one revolution of the pedals equalled one revolution of the wheel. In the case of the 'ordinary' (Penny Farthing) type of machine, where the front wheel was very large, this meant very high gearing, so the machine was not suitable for hill climbs of any marked gradient. With the advent of the 'safety' cycle, where the wheels were of smaller, similar dimensions, with the rider seated between them, transmitting power to the rear wheel via a chain drive, gearing became possible.

Other features which we now take for granted were also once innovations. The rear wheel, rather than being driven by a fixed cog which revolved at all times, forcing the rider's feet round, was freed, allowing 'coasting' downhill. At first this was achieved by the simple expedient of putting foot-rests on the forward part of the frame, so the feet could be merely lifted off the pedals during a descent. Later, the cog itself was constructed with a ratchet arrangement which locked during forward

motion, but freed it when forward motion was not applied. This was known as the 'freewheel' and is the basis of all variable cycle transmission systems today.

The next major development was to supply several gears to suit different terrain. This led to the introduction of the hub gearing system which survives to the present day on those machines equipped with a 'Sturmey Archer' type of hub gear – where a miniature gearbox arrangement is housed within the wheel hub, giving three or four different drive ratios. This is mainly confined to heavy roadsters or shopping bikes. It is a very reliable form of gearing, but of limited use for anything other than urban riding and commuting, and completely out of place on a serious off-road bicycle. The transmission system which made the mountain bike possible was derived from the 'derailleur' mechanisms developed for touring.

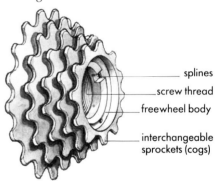

splines
screw thread
freewheel body

interchangeable
sprockets (cogs)

Freewheel block

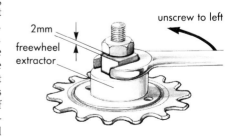

unscrew to left

2mm
freewheel
extractor

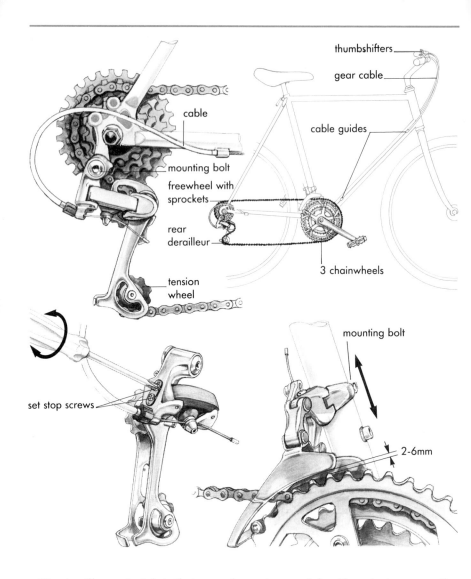

thumbshifters

gear cable

cable

cable guides

mounting bolt

freewheel with
sprockets

rear
derailleur

3 chainwheels

tension
wheel

set stop screws

mounting bolt

2-6mm

The derailleur principle is that several (five or seven) cogs are mounted on a freewheel block on the rear wheel, and a long chain travels over the selected cog, through a tensioning and shifting device, which moves the chain sideways from one cog to another, taking up the loose chain or paying out more to compensate for larger or smaller cogs. Racing-type derailleurs work over 'close-ratio' gear blocks with less variation in cog size, and have smaller tensioning devices.

A second derailleur device moves the chain across two or three chainwheels, giving a range of between ten and twenty-one different gear ratios. However, in practice fifteen- or eighteen-speed models are common with mountain bikes, and often the number of ratios used is rather less, since it is not wise practice to use the smallest chainwheel and the smallest cog, or the largest chainwheel and cog, since the way the mechanism is laid out makes for very acute angles in the chain

Typical mountain bike gearing ratios

Number of teeth on chainwheel

Teeth on sprocket	24	26	28	30	32	34	36	38	39	40	41	42	43	44	45	46	47	48	49	50	51	52	53
13	48	52	56	60	64	68	72	76	78	80	82	84	86	88	90	92	94	96	98	100	102	104	106
14	45	48	52	56	60	63	67	70	72	74	76	78	80	82	84	85	87	89	91	93	95	97	98
15	42	45	49	52	55	59	62	66	68	69	71	73	75	76	78	80	81	83	85	87	88	90	92
16	39	42	45	49	52	55	58	61	63	65	67	68	70	72	73	75	76	78	80	81	83	85	86
17	37	40	43	46	49	52	55	58	60	61	63	64	66	67	69	70	72	73	75	76	78	80	81
18	35	38	40	43	46	49	52	55	56	58	59	61	62	64	65	66	68	69	71	72	74	75	77
19	33	36	38	41	44	47	49	52	53	55	56	57	59	60	62	63	64	66	67	68	70	71	73
20	31	34	36	39	42	44	47	49	51	52	53	55	56	57	59	60	61	62	64	65	66	68	69
21	30	32	35	37	40	42	45	47	48	50	51	52	53	54	56	57	58	59	61	62	63	64	66
22	28	31	33	35	38	40	43	45	46	47	48	50	51	52	53	54	56	57	58	59	60	61	63
23	27	29	32	34	36	38	41	43	44	45	46	47	49	50	51	52	53	54	55	57	58	59	60
24	26	28	30	32	35	37	39	41	42	43	44	45	47	48	49	50	51	52	53	54	55	56	57
25	25	27	29	31	33	35	37	39	41	42	43	44	45	46	47	48	49	50	51	52	53	54	55
26	24	26	28	30	32	34	36	38	39	40	41	42	43	44	45	46	47	48	49	50	51	52	53
27	23	25	27	29	31	33	35	37	38	39	39	40	41	42	43	44	45	46	47	48	49	50	51
28	22	24	26	28	30	32	33	35	36	37	38	39	40	41	42	43	44	45	46	46	47	48	49
30	21	23	24	26	28	29	31	33	34	35	36	36	37	38	39	40	41	42	42	43	44	45	46
32	20	21	23	24	26	28	29	31	32	33	33	34	35	35	37	37	38	39	40	41	41	42	43
34	18	20	21	23	24	26	28	29	30	31	31	32	33	33	34	35	36	37	37	38	39	40	41
38	16	18	19	21	22	23	25	26	27	27	28	29	29	30	31	31	32	32	33	34	35	36	36

Number of teeth on sprocket

Typical mountain bike gearing ratios

line, and this causes excessive wear and risks breakage. However, the mountain biker still has a very usable range of sixteen speeds, ranging from very low ratios, for climbing all but the most vertical ascents, through to moderately high gears for use on made-up roads. The lower gears also have the effect of providing 'instant' controllable power, a most useful asset when you are man-œuvring the machine around rocks, or along slippery paths.

The ratio of a gear is the relationship between the chainwheel, sprocket and wheel diameter combination. The for-mula is:

indexed shifter

$$\frac{\text{no. teeth on chainwheel} \times \text{wheel diameter (inches)}}{\text{no. teeth on rear sprocket}} = \text{ratio}$$

non-indexed shifter

The ratio is expressed in inches, and is the forward travel obtained for a single revolution of the chainwheel. The chart on page 63 shows the ratios obtainable on a typical mountain bike with varying chainwheel/rear sprocket combinations.

On mountain bikes, the control levers are 'thumbshifters' mounted on the handlebars, so that gears can be changed without relinquishing any control of the machine. Nowadays, these are 'indexed', or provided with positive click stops for each gear position, which makes gear shifting a very safe and predictable action. The levers are connected by Bowden cables to the front and rear derailleurs.

Suntour and Shimano are the manu-facturers whose wide-range derailleurs seem to have gained the largest share of the US and, increasingly, the European market. Good products are also avail-able from European manufacturers such as Simplex, and Campagnolo announced a new system for mountain bikes in 1988. Specific 'ATB' shift mechanisms are available now from Shi-mano and Suntour, and these are, with-out doubt, very effective products. They take a remarkable amount of strain and abuse, and many of the mechanisms are

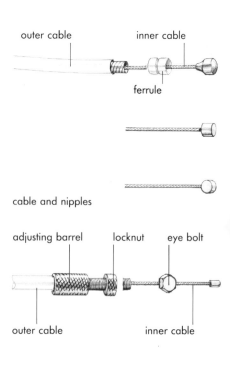

outer cable   inner cable

ferrule

cable and nipples

adjusting barrel   locknut   eye bolt

outer cable   inner cable

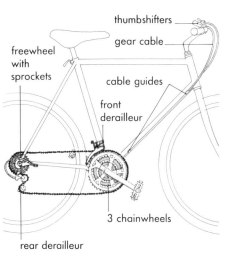

thumbshifters

gear cable

freewheel
with
sprockets

cable guides

front
derailleur

3 chainwheels

rear derailleur

front derailleur

protected by a metal guard to fend off the worst blows from rocks and roots. This is probably a wise investment, since the amount of damage that can be inflicted when a derailleur intrudes into a revolving spoked wheel is really quite impressive.

The chain is driven by the chainwheels, usually a set of three, attached to aluminium cranks connected by a spline and bolt arrangement to the axle in the bottom bracket. Such chainwheels are an expensive component, often supplied in a grouped set of matching accessories. Again, Shimano and Suntour are prominent and well respected in this area, although other manufacturers – TA, Campagnolo, Stronglight, and so on, also supply good products.

There has been some innovation in this area recently. 'Biopace' chainwheels by Shimano were introduced with eccentric chainrings, which the manufacturer claimed removed the high-resistance 'top dead centre' point from the pedalling action, and they have become widely accepted. Browning in the US offer a revolutionary product, where a segment of the chainwheel is make to slope by an electronic control device, making for a very smooth change, even under pressure.

▶ Chains and sprockets ◀

These much-abused components are at the heart of the transmission system and should be of the highest quality you can afford to avoid irritating breakdowns. Already mentioned is the cassetted type of rear sprocket block made by Shimano, which offers great convenience to those few riders who wish to change ratios frequently. In practice, a good strong standard screwthread-type block suffices, married to a recognized branded chain. It is seldom that a manufacturer will seek foolish economies in this area, for whilst the items are relatively inexpensive, failures will immobilize the entire machine.

You should give the transmission

system the greatest attention when maintaining the mountain bike. It takes the most strain of all the moving parts, and is completely open to the elements – grit, dust and random knocks from trailside obstacles. Also, when riding along paths fringed by long grass, you can collect a build-up of vegetation between the sprockets which will eventually make it impossible for the chain to grip, and a messy few minutes will have to be spent in removing the offending flora.

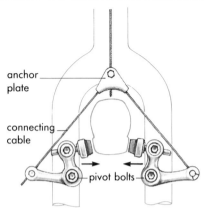

anchor plate

connecting cable

pivot bolts

Cantilever brake

▶BRAKES ◀

It is not always appreciated that efficient brakes are one of the greatest contributions to high performance and out-and-out speed on any cycle. A rider with complete confidence in the steed's ability to stop on demand is able to approach corners and obstacles at a higher terminal speed, spending less time decelerating and accelerating than would be the case with inefficient 'stoppers'.

The brakes used on today's mountain bikes are derived from the cantilever type used on tandems, and are very reliable if you use them in conjunction with good, composite-material brake blocks, and adjust them correctly. At least, this is true where the cantilevers are fitted front and rear, and mounted out of the way of dust, grit and mud. It is certainly true of most front assemblies, since the front of the fork crown is the only practical mounting for a brake. Regrettably, there has been a tendency to use 'U-brakes' – in themselves a perfectly sound design – for the rear brake, mounted under the chainstay. As was pointed out above, this fixing-point is particularly vulnerable to dirt and wet. This also makes brake maintenance more difficult, and in my opinion would be sufficient grounds to influence your choice towards a model with rear callipers, or a U-brake mounted up on the seat stay – the proper position.

The early mountain bikes were fitted with coaster brakes – enclosed assemb-

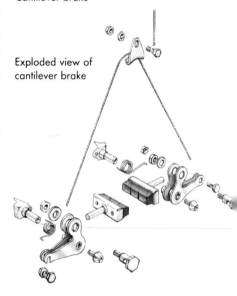

Exploded view of cantilever brake

lies which are basically similar to the drum brake on a car. In theory, the drum brake has advantages, since it is totally enclosed, and should perform equally well in all weathers. Indeed, some very specialized machinery, particularly many custom-made mountain bikes use very sophisticated light-alloy drum brakes to great effect. However, to be good, such components usually have also to be very expensive, and they can have other drawbacks – such as more complex maintenance requirements – and of course, if a wheel

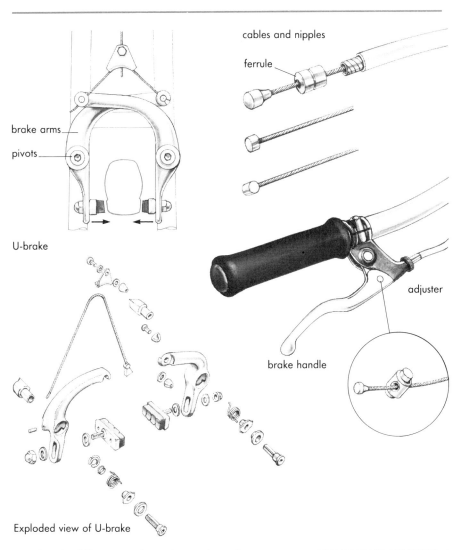

cables and nipples

ferrule

brake arms

pivots

U-brake

adjuster

brake handle

Exploded view of U-brake

needs rebuilding, you lose the entire braking system, unless you have a spare which is similarly equipped.

Most riders will be pinning their safety to the calliper front and cantilever or U-brake rear set-up which, if you make sure that brake blocks are well adjusted and renewed frequently, wheel rims are true and their braking surfaces intact, will provide sufficient braking power to stop the bike in a relatively straight line and a remarkably short distance.

▶AN OVER-ENGINEERED FREAK?◀

These, then, are the major components of the mountain bike. There are those who would argue that many of the parts or design features are unnecessary, or that the whole machine is over-engineered for the task it is called upon to perform. After all, have not cycle tourists been taking perfectly standard machines off-road for years, and have they not managed to keep their bikes in one piece?

This opinion, while valid, misses an

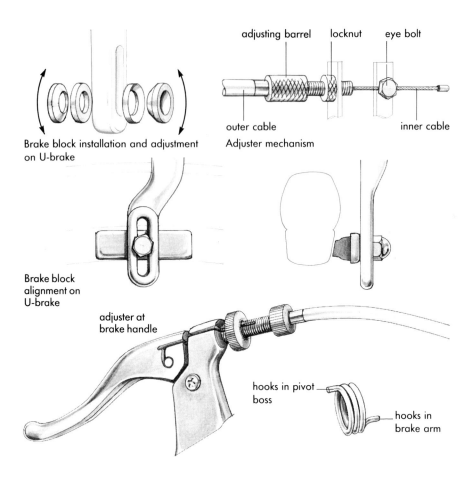

adjusting barrel   locknut   eye bolt

outer cable   inner cable

Brake block installation and adjustment on U-brake

Adjuster mechanism

Brake block alignment on U-brake

adjuster at brake handle

hooks in pivot boss

hooks in brake arm

essential point. A piece of equipment must not only be well designed for the task it has to perform. If it is to be successful, it should also capture the imagination and stimulate the desire to use it for ever more challenging tasks. High-performance motor cars do not have to look streamlined and sleek, but those which have made history always have. This is also true of the mountain bike. The fact is that oversize frame tubing, unicrown forks, huge knobbly tyres and titanium handlebars may not be strictly required for most cycling, but they have attracted more people to the sport than the industry can remember for many a year.

Off-road cycling has taken off with people of all ages, and the mountain bike has been the lever. No doubt the specification outlined here will evolve, but it has been a starting-point of great value, and there can be no denying that mountain bikes have put adventure, fun and an appreciation of the value of healthy exercise away from the frustrations and dangers of our roads, into the grasp of thousands. That is an acheivement to outweigh the petty technical carping of the purists, any day.

The popularity of the mountain bike has been so immediate and widespread that there are many people who buy one as their first serious bike, and who may not have acquired riding skills beyond those basic to juvenile cycling. Of course, many riders are serious cyclists, and take up mountain biking as a further dimension to their sport; or they may be pretty hot off-road performers already, having just graduated from a BMX.

This section is for the novice rider, who, having acquired an ATB, needs to gain proficiency in the basic skills before progressing to the more advanced manœuvres.

▸SET-UP AND POSTURE◂

Good riding begins even before you commit yourself to the bike of your choice. It is true of buying any bicycle that unless the machine is within a size range which suits the individual rider, not only will it fail to give its best performance, it may even be dangerous. This is even more true of the mountain bike, for machine and rider will be encountering more challenges than they do in routine cycling, and they need to operate as a single unit.

The question of fit has been mentioned before, but it is worth repeating that mountain bike frames should be

Good posture is the key to control

around 2.5 inches smaller than standard road bikes, allowing about 4 inches between crotch and top tube when you stand astride the bike with both feet flat on the ground. This is to minimize painful contact between rider and top tube in event of a spill, but it also permits the wide range of saddle and stem adjustments which may be necessary to deal with extended riding over various types of terrain. For instance, long descents over rough ground are best accomplished with the saddle lowered and extended backwards. You can't acheive that and still exercise control over the machine if the frame is too big.

Any good dealer will make sizing the frame the first step in selling the bike. However, it's likely that some shops, less familiar with the mountain bike and its particular foibles, will be unaware of this basic fact, and will tend to the practice of suggesting a larger frame, citing 'room for growth' in a youngster as justification. Don't be deterred. Look

Mountain bike frames are some 2 to 2.5 inches smaller than their road counterparts

Mountain bike seat and handlebar stems allow ample adjustment

at any of the competition photos in the mountain biking mags, and you will see that the top riders are all on machines significantly smaller than those used on the road. Mountain bike components are specially engineered to allow sufficient extension of saddle pin and stem, and these items are supplied over-long to provide safety at all practical ranges of adjustment. If you are buying for a youngster, and he or she appears likely to be seduced by the dealer's 'That's a kid's frame, you need something bigger', leave the shop, buy a copy of *Bicycle Action* and turn to the mountain bike pages to satisfy Junior's doubts, and then look in the index or at the ads to find a nearby shop where they do know what they are talking about!

Of course, mere size of frame isn't the only consideration. As we have seen, frame geometry dictates the length of individual tubes, and this will affect your posture on the bike. Posture is important because it determines rider comfort, wind resistance and the force

which can be brought to bear on pedalling.

It's frequently assumed that, because mountain bikes have straight bars, an upright posture is required. This is wrong. The purpose of straight or slightly upswept bars is to give better vision and to provide a surface on which you can reach all the various braking and gear-changing controls quickly and without taking your hands off the grips. A straight-backed, vertical posture won't allow you to achieve efficiency or comfort, and you need something nearer the crouched style affected by the long-distance tourer or racer. In fact, such a posture is far more relaxed and comfortable, because the rider's weight is spread evenly between the bars and saddle, so avoiding numbness, or even damage, to the posterior. It also enables you to transfer weight very quickly by getting out of the saddle – either to exert maximum force down on the pedals, or to slide back and 'hang the tail out' for hazardous descents. The ability to change balance, centre of gravity and working position is important on any bike, vital on an ATB.

The mountain biker decreases wind-resistance by bending the arms and leaning more. Of course, dropped handlebars make for a more extreme crouch than do the straights fitted to mountain bikes, but most riders, even when racing, spend the greater part of their riding time either holding the flat top portion of the bars, or, more often, with their hands over the hoods of the brakes. The drops are used only in a sprint, or when minimum wind resistance is essential. Indeed, for some road and track purposes, the handlebars of racing machines have now been adapted by removing the lower portion of the drops altogether. For mountain bikers, wind resistance is less of a performance factor off-road, where traction, manœuvrability and simply staying on board are more important than the streamlining sought by the time-trial racer on tarmac.

▶ Saddles and seating position ◀

Probably the most critical dimension of the mountain bike is saddle height. It impinges on comfort, safety and performance, and is the first factor you should fix when selecting a machine. With children, it is a point to check and adjust regularly, until they stop growing.

The simplest and most effective way to check and fix saddle height accurately is to sit on the bike with the height set roughly to allow you to reach the ground on both sides with the balls of your feet. You should wear the shoes which you will have on most frequently for cycling. Position the bike alongside a wall and, leaning with your right hand on the wall for support, move the left pedal backwards to its lowest point. Your left heel should be on the pedal, and the height of the saddle adjusted so that your leg is straight, but not stretched. Turning the bike round, repeat the procedure for the other foot and then, holding the machine as near vertical as possible, pedal backwards (still using your heels) to ensure that it is possible to revolve the cranks completely without shifting from side to side in the saddle. Finally, measure the difference between the height of your heels and your soles (usually a fraction of an inch) and lower the saddle by that amount. You should now be able to rotate the cranks without strain at all times – and put a foot down easily to support the bike when you're stopping – provided you bought the right size of frame in the first place.

Ideally you should have gone through this procedure in the cycle shop before you bought the bike. Almost all the other dimensions of a bike are less critical than this one, and failure to find the right saddle height will seriously depress your enjoyment of the bike. In an extreme case, it could lead to a nasty accident. These days, manufacturers are offering quite a variety of frame geometries with ATBs, so knowing that the boy next door had a 19.5 inch frame is not enough to go on –

it may have a different bottom-bracket height, and that will affect sizing. And if you can only get the right saddle height with the saddle at its lowest fixing, then it is a completely unsuitable machine, since that won't allow the essential clearance between one of your softer bits and a chrome-steel top-tube!

Of course, having ascertained the right saddle height and firmly fixed the seat pin (either with the binder bolt or, more commonly, with the quick-release mechanism), you have to adjust the *rake* of the saddle as well, before you can do any serious road-testing. The rake, or 'tilt', has a great effect on comfort. It is often mistakenly believed that the nose of the saddle should be tilted up to 'anchor' the rider more firmly, and give something to pull against. This is a dangerous fiction – in fact, the high-points of peak and seat must be exactly aligned in the horizontal plane, and the saddle itself very firmly tightened to prevent any movement under stress.

Wrongly tilted saddles can lead to a painful numbness, which – in its most extreme form – can last for days. It is essential for a mountain bike rider to be able easily to shift position when riding, and almost nothing can equal the surprise and agony of sitting down hard on a saddle which has moved during a traverse of rough ground, and now offers only the pointed end as you sink back, expecting comfort and support.

There is one other vital adjustment: the saddle will also move backwards and forwards. The right position is one where your knee is over the pedal centre, when the pedal is in its most forward position in the horizontal plane.

Once you've determined the theoretically correct saddle height, you need to test the hypothesis in practice, over the kind of terrain you are normally going to ride, for perhaps a thousand miles or so, and make minor adjustments until you find the most comfortable seat.

Then mark the stem with an indelible spirit marker of some kind to make it easy to return quickly to the optimum if you move the saddle later. If you're likely to make frequent adjustments to saddle height – and this will certainly be the case for any sustained off-road riding – it's a good idea to fit one of the saddle-adjustment aids, such as Hite-Rite, which take the strain out of raising and lowering the saddle.

▶ Position on the pedals ◀

Foot position on the pedals is another consideration. Pedals are driven by the balls of your feet, and it's important to ensure that you have good location here, to gain the most thrust, to avoid ankle strain, and to position yourself most advantageously.

Good foot location is fairly simple to achieve with the type of pedal fitted to most mountain bikes, if you are wearing trainers. If you go all the way and use proper mountain bike shoes (as yet, ruinously expensive) and toe-clips, good positioning is assured. Another advantage of toe-clips is that they aid pedalling efficiency by allowing the rider to exert power during more of the crank revolution, which is certainly an advantage to much off-road work. On the other hand, having your feet secured to the pedals could cause you problems in a spill... The use of toe-clips is an individual decision, but most serious rough-terrain riders will prob-ably fit them eventually.

▶ Handlebar height and reach ◀

Handlebars allow another posture adjustment. You can raise or lower the handlebar stem, twist the bars in the stem to alter the tilt and angle of the grips and, as a final resort, you can saw bits off the ends of the bars to reduce the width. This last measure is useful either for adapting a bike for use mainly in town, where narrow gaps are to be frequently negotiated, or where a smaller rider finds the spread of his or her arms uncomfortable.

The height of the bars obviously has an effect on both the posture or crouch of the rider and the field of vision. Positions vary between level with the saddle, and 1 or 2 inches below it, depending on individual preference. Different reaches can be obtained by varying the length of the stem, and there are certainly plenty to choose from. Frame size, once again, will have an effect on this choice, but, broadly speaking, with the saddle correctly

*To make adjustments, loosen the binder bolt
and raise or lower the stem*

positioned, you should be able to reach
the binder bolt of the stem with your
middle finger, when your elbow is
touching the saddle peak. If you can't,
then the frame is too large overall or, in
the case of short-armed riders, if the
frame height is correct, you need a
shorter top tube. You may have to
consult a specialist mountain bike
dealer, who will browse through manufacturers' catalogues with you, or – as a

last resort – you may need a custom-
built frame. (Mind you, if you have the
money, there is nothing nicer than a
hand-built bike made to your own
specifications.) A problem you will
seldom find is having the top tube
slightly too short. Stems come in a
variety of lengths and types, and many
are upswept to allow for the smaller
frame-sizing of ATBs.

Unless you have already used a
mountain bike extensively, and have a
very definite idea about your preferred
riding position, don't specify a different

Stem adjustments may necessitate compensatory adjustments to the brake mechanism

stem from the one which is fitted to a stock bike, even if it seems fashionable. The stem plays a part in more than just positioning the bars; it often has a cable guide for the front brake, and in some systems is an integral part of the brake. Likewise, some stem–bar combinations are designed to be used together, and swapping one or the other may affect the performance of the steering unit as a whole. So a decision to exchange the perfectly serviceable upswept aluminium stem for the pink fluorescent steel job might turn out more expensive than you thought.

Adjustment of these items is fairly simple, although you have to proceed with care to avoid unsightly scratches, particularly with aluminium components. To loosen the stem, unscrew the expander bolt until about a half-inch is projecting and then, protecting the bolt top with a piece of hard wood, tap it sharply with a hammer to push the

Hand spacing on the bars should not exceed shoulder width

expander cone out of the end of the stem inside the head tube. Then, standing astride the front wheel and facing the saddle, lift the stem, holding the ends of the bars, until you reach the desired height. Tighten the expander bolt again. In those stems where the front brake cable is involved, you may also need to adjust your front brakes now. (Manufacturers leave a long cable for this very reason.) Don't be tempted to trim it for the sake of appearance, or you may achieve the right position only to find that you have lost all braking power on the front wheel!

You may want to experiment with the tilt and angle of the bars, either to make the grips more comfortable to hold or to fine-tune the reach (bearing in mind that this may well affect the height and call for a readjustment of the stem). The handlebar is clamped in the stem by the action of one or more binder bolts, which may be combined with a spline on the inside of the clamp, engaging with a similarly engraved set of grooves on the bars themselves. If you do have a spline, be sure to loosen the bolts

sufficiently to enable the bar to rotate freely, otherwise you may damage the spline. This is particularly a risk with a combination of steel and alloy for stem and bar.

As a general rule, the distance between your hands on the bars should not greatly exceed your shoulder width. It is quite a false belief that the wide-spread 'cowhorn' type of bar seen on 'easy rider' motorbikes improves steering efficiency off-road. The opposite is the case, and such monstrosities merely provide one more hazard for the rider to be impaled on when involuntarily dismounting. The environment provides enough such hazards – don't have the bars any wider than absolutely necessary.

When you put all these points together, you will find that a good riding position will place your shoulders more or less midway between your hands and buttocks, which means they are approximately over the bottom-bracket of the machine. Individual riders may prefer small variations, but most will settle into a position like this, finding that it provides the perfect combination of comfort and control.

Once you find your optimum position, you can only really test it by getting a lot of miles in, both on- and off-road. Inevitably, some minor niggles will show up at this stage, primarily saddle soreness and aching wrists.

Saddle soreness

This afflicts *all* inexperienced cyclists in the first week or two of riding and, providing the machine is in good adjustment, you have obtained the right posture, and you have a good saddle in level alignment, it will go away, as the muscles and tissues involved get the message. If it doesn't, suspect the saddle. If it's plastic, then perhaps you would do better with one of the leather-covered anatomical sorts. If you are feeling particularly tender, it might be that you would be best served by one of the all-leather, sprung Brooks saddles

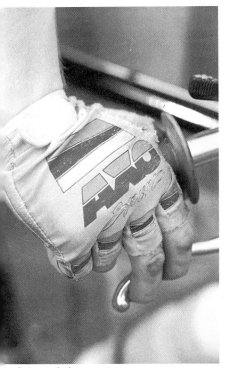

Grips and gloves

– they now have a specialist mountain bike model – but even this won't provide an instant answer, because they need to be worn-in before they are truly comfortable. After that, though, they are a joy. (Remember that leather is an organic material and will require regular proofing with saddle soap or gel; this will also aid the wearing-in process.)

It's as well to make a good saddle a priority when you are buying a first bike. Some riders keep the one saddle for life, transferring it between the machines, and there is much to commend the practice. It is a sad fact that some quite high-priced machines economize on saddles, and that should be avoided.

Aching wrists

You may get some discomfort in your wrists, and find numbness in the palms of your hands. This is usually due to the tendons of the wrist reacting to un-accustomed strain and they will soon adapt. The numbness may come because you have not yet fully relaxed on the bike and are putting too much force on arms and hands, rather than riding 'from the hips'; this will come in time. If it doesn't, suspect first your riding position, and check that your shoulders are midway between the bars and saddle. If that's not the answer, try altering the angle of the bars, and if that doesn't work, fit soft foam grips ('Grab-Ons', for example), and use a good brand of ATB riding gloves.

In nearly every case, the aches and pains of unaccustomed exercise and strain will vanish very quickly, as long as the rider learns the other techniques of good riding which are covered in the rest of this section. A word of caution, however. If, after persevering and trying the remedies offered here, you still experience pain or discomfort, then consult a doctor. Cycling is one of the most natural and healthy exercises known to humankind, practised painlessly by peoples in every country of the world. It should not hurt! If it does, either you are doing something

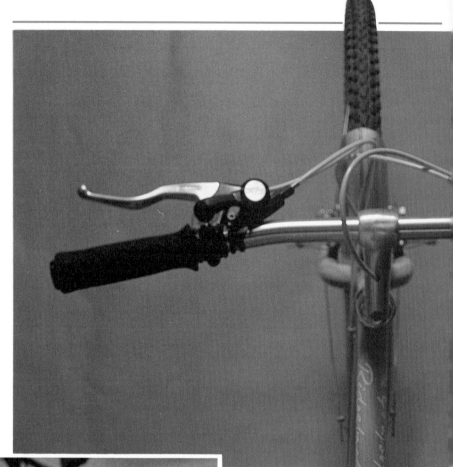

wrong, your equipment is at fault, or you have a physical problem which should be attended to promptly by a doctor.

▶USING THE CONTROLS◀

Mountain bikes differ from other machines more in their layout than in

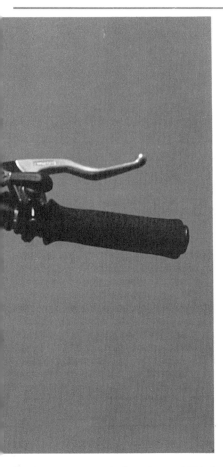

small space. When a light bracket and a small on-board computer monitoring everything from m.p.h. to heartbeat are added, the novice rider can be forgiven some confusion. Sort out what the various levers do, before you take to the trail!

On the right handlebar are positioned the front brake lever, with its built-in cable adjuster, and the thumb-shifter for the rear (five- or six-speed) derailleur. The left bar houses the rear brake and front (two- or three-speed) derailleur. Just to complicate matters further, it is usual to pull the rear (right-hand) derailleur control towards you for higher gears, while the same operation on the front (left-hand) derailleur finds lower gears. In practice, you soon learn this, and a mistake isn't serious, since it results only in your finding it harder to pedal when you were expecting some relief from a lower gear. Such experiences soon encourage the beginner to change gears early, and that is anyway one of the first principles of successful mountain bike riding!

▶Braking◀

The brakes are less forgiving than gears to the inexperienced. You have to understand the concept of weight transfer, in its simplest sense, to be able to operate brakes efficiently on any kind of bike, and most particularly on a mountain bike, where they play such a part in the whole riding process. The effect on any braking force applied to the wheels of a cycle travelling in a forward direction is to restrain the velocity of the machine, while the rider continues to have forward momentum. This results in a transfer of weight forward and down which, if not properly managed, results first in an almost total lack of traction on the rear wheel, and then in a tendency for the rider to be catapulted over the front of the machine.

Since that is obviously undesirable, we compensate by using sensitive pressure on the brakes, rather than jamming them on and hoping for the

the type or amount of equipment fitted. True, many of the components have been adapted to the special requirements of off-road riding, but still, there are plenty of touring machines with fifteen or eighteen gears; centre-pull and cantilever brakes are not unique to the ATB. The main distinguishing design feature of a mountain bike is that it has been constructed to give the rider the ability to manipulate every control without shifting hands from handlebar grips.

This obviously sensible facility is achieved by positioning thumb-shifter levers for the front and rear derailleurs adjacent to – or in some cases making them part of – the brake levers. While it is both convenient and practical, this does site an awful lot of equipment in a

The out-of-saddle rider is in a better position to make the split-second transfers of weight necessary in maintaining balance

best, and by alternating use of front and rear brake according to circumstance. For example, when you're riding on an ordinary road with a good, dry surface and normal tyre adhesion, it is best to 'lead' with the front brake to make the main reduction of speed, and then progressively increase the pressure of your rear brake so that the retarding force on both wheels is steadiy increased, without ever encouraging a skid. This is exactly what 'ABS' (anti-lock braking) systems do on cars, by acting to release pressure momentarily before the wheels lock up. However, cars have computers to help them, whereas humans must rely on experience, so it's sensible to test the braking performance of a new bike on a quiet road before embarking on any major journeys.

The same is true for off-road riding, as the machine really comes into its own here, and will behave in a way which feels quite different from the stable docility you find in most mountain bikes on tarmac. The main difference for the novice off-road is the need to reduce dependence on the front brake as the main retarding force. Whereas on tarmac the object is to minimize skidding, off-road, especially in the wet, this is impossible, and so skidding has to be managed. In such circumstances, you soon realize that the chances of recovering from a rear wheel slide are fairly good, while 'losing' the front wheel can be much more serious!

▶ Gears ◀

Gears are often referred to as 'speeds'. This is misleading, since the only determinants of speed are gradient, wind resistance and work-rate. (In theory, friction plays a part too, but this is really only significant as a factor on smooth surfaces, so you can discount it for mountain biking.) The real purpose of gearing is to make the 'work' easier by permitting a greater number of pedal revolutions per wheel revolution, thus easing the muscular strain needed to cope with the gradient. In fact, your objective when cycling should be to maintain as constant a speed as possible. It is also more efficient for the human body to maintain a fairly steady 'cadence', or pedalling rate, throughout any journey, and variable gearing helps to achieve that.

Everybody has their own ideal cadence – for most of us, somewhere between 60 and 80 r.p.m. is the norm. Because you are likely to come across such a wide range of gradients, mountain bikes are equipped with a very wide range of gears, from extremely low, to medium-high (see pages 61-6). The most common beginner's mistake is to select too high a gear, in the belief that it will mean faster progress. While that may be true for the first couple of miles, fatigue sets in rapidly, accompanied in the inexperienced by various muscular pains, and overall journey time – not to mention enjoyment – suffers. Even racing cyclists select lower gears than they are actually capable of pushing, some pedalling to a cadence of 100 r.p.m. or more.

For mountain bikes, the 'lower gear than you can push' rule is even more important, because on rough terrain the rider is constantly encountering undulations which, if they coincide with 'top dead centre', which is the point of greatest inertia in the pedalling cycle, can bring a machine and a rider in too high a gear to a dead halt. The eccentric chainwheel (see page 65) is supposed to minimize this effect, but in practice the only remedy is to anticipate obstacles and always select a sufficiently low gear in plenty of time.

Gear selection with thumb-shifters is quite a simple operation but you will find that a little sensitivity works wonders. Most of the gear sets fitted to today's mountain bikes are 'indexed' – that is, they have click stops or ratchets which positively locate each gear position. This doesn't mean that with a quick wrench from gear to gear the machinery will sort itself out. The derailleur system is a fairly crude device, highly stressed and engineered to the limits of performance of the materials from which it is constructed. Its principle of operation is that it moves the chain out of alignment with the cog upon which it is engaged so that the chain link meshes with a tooth of the next cog and is pulled on to it by the revolution of the cog. The system only works because the chain flexes sideways, and it is axiomatic that if something flexes, it also wears. The rate of wear is grossly exaggerated by insensitive gear-changing, and the trick is to ease off your pressure on the pedals as you make the change. You can pretty easily hear the difference between a scarcely perceptible click and a graunch signifying the loss of another two weeks' chain life.

The front derailleur, which swaps the chain between chainwheels, and is operated by the left thumb-shifter, is usually a rather more difficult proposition than the rear gears, since the machinery is even more primitive. It consists of a cage through which the chain runs, which pushes the chain so that it either drops on to the smaller ring or is pressed against the outer, larger chainring until finally a tooth gets some purchase on a bit of the chain and hauls it up on to the circumference of the toothed chainwheel. The potential for wear is enormous, as the steel sideplates of the shift mechanism make contact with the chain, and the outer links of the chain with the inner surfaces of the toothed rings. It's a wonder the contraption works at all, and it is certainly not one of our more elegant inventions. With the rear gears, then, it is even more important not to change under pressure, and you should remember that a high pedalling rate combined with a momentary easing of pressure is a great help when you change to a higher ratio (bigger chainwheel).

It is worth noting here that the Browning triple chainwheel which is fitted as standard to the latest top-of-the range Specialized bikes uses an entirely different system of changing, where a section of the chainring itself is moved

by an electronically operated relay, and this provides much more positive and sophisticated changes. The system still has to prove itself over a long period in practice, but it is fitted to some professional racing machinery, so coming competition seasons will tell whether this is a long-awaited breakthrough.

One final tip. It should be obvious that it's not a good idea to start off in a high gear, so, as with driving a car, get used to coming down through the ratios as your journey ends, so that the bike is in an appropriate gear for a quiet and trouble-free start.

▶Steering◀

Steering is effected by a combination of turning the bars and leaning in the desired direction of travel ... most of the time.

The exception to this rule is when a quick, rather than smooth, change of direction is required, in which case a brief turn of the bars in the opposite direction produces a faster lean into the turn than would otherwise be possible. This is a technique that is very useful to the mountain bike rider, both off-road and on the obstacle courses which pass as main thouroughfares in most major cities. The skill of weaving with precision and safety is paramount in all cycling, and when you are stomping along at speed through woodland or down mountain slopes, it needs to be second nature.

The steer and lean actions are not mutually exclusive! At any speed at all, if you merely turn the bars, without the corrective lean in the same direction, it will result in the machine falling over on to the side opposite the direction of the turn. The process is one of constant correction and counter-correction, which – if a rider has any aptitude at all – quickly becomes second nature. This has to happen if you are to gain any degree of proficiency off-road, for here the rules are often broken, and special techniques are developed to get bike and rider over broken and difficult terrain. But in the beginning, it's important to develop a familiarity with the machine on a good surface which enables tight and precise control, particularly during low-speed manœuvres.

Another point to remember throughout your cycling life (simply because failure to do so may abruptly terminate it!) is that cyclists are able to react much faster than other road users, and this ability is more marked as the size-weight ratio increases. The stopping time of a bus is incomparably slower than that of a bike, even when they are travelling at the same speed, simply because a bus has so much more weight

to arrest. It is also true of turning, and therefore the cyclist has a great responsibility for his or her own safety. Defensive riding involves clear signalling of your intention, developing the skills of observation and anticipation and having a sense of the unseen, both behind you and lurking in drives and round corners.

Good cyclists always have somewhere to go in an emergency – preferably somewhere other vehicles,

especially heavy ones, can't get. While such instincts are less necessary in the backwoods, most mountain bikers ride the roads to get to their favourite trail, and good traffic skills are a basic requirement. *Cyclecraft* by John Franklin, and the wonderful *Richard's Bicycle Book* by Richard Ballantine – a classic in its own right – can be obtained cheaply from any good bookshop, and may save your life many times over without you ever realizing it.

Even off-road, common sense allied to logical anticipation will often mean the difference between being invited to join a bunch of like-minded mountain bikers on a 'thrash' and being left to find your own trails. No one likes following an unpredictable rider, and there is often less room in the rough stuff for others to compensate for a careless rider's sudden stops and changes of direction.

▶THE FIRST RIDE◀

Once you've established a good position, become familiar with the controls, checked to see that saddle, bars, brakes, wheels and all vital bolts and quick-release levers are properly secured, (which the dealer should also do), it is time for the first ride. Even on a mountain bike, you should make the first journey on a metalled road, preferably a quiet close or cul-de-sac, and use the ride to test all the bike's controls and systems. Choose a dry, clear day and be thorough in your exploration of these points. No matter that the local heath beckons, or that there are friends to be impressed with the new bike; the most important task is to obtain a working familiarity with the machine.

▶ Testing brakes ◀

First, establish the points at which the rear wheel locks up under heavy braking and find the degree of pressure on the front brake required to make the rear end of the bike feel light and skittish – which is the prelude to a brief and painful trip over the bars.

Select a fairly low gear and wind the bike up to a moderate speed. Apply the rear brake alone, increasing the pressure gradually until the rear wheel locks, then release the brake at once. Now repeat the experiment, but this time apply the front brake first, using moderate pressure only, and a moment later start applying the rear brake. Now progressively increase the pressure on both brakes simultaneously, staying ready to slacken off the moment there is any sign of lock-up on the rear. The result – of course – will be that the stopping distance over that achieved with the rear brake alone will be dramatically decreased, without a sign of a skid. Practise this 'emergency stop' until the action is second nature, varying the speed at which the operation is performed, both in terms of the bike's velocity and of application of braking pressure. This will establish the

optimum braking performance of the machine on good roads in fair weather, and provide the limits of safety, which you should always know. From this you can calculate the shortest possible stopping distance at any given speed.

Remember that the back brake is really only a drag. Alone, it cannot stop the cycle in anything like an efficient manner but, as a trimmer, to check speed on fast descents or on a fast approach to a bend, it can be used with great subtlety once you master it.

In wet weather, of course, things change. Much greater stopping distances must be allowed, both to ensure that you can use lighter braking pressures to prevent slip and skidding, and to overcome the fact that wet rims are far less effective braking surfaces. (This is worse on steel rims than aluminium, but any machine supplied with steel rims is not worthy of the name mountain bike.)

In any event, a good rider will be aware of the stopping potential of the bike in all weathers and on all surfaces, but will not need to use that potential very often; good anticipation should mean that you rarely need to bring the machine to a complete halt. More often, braking is used to check progress, and ensure that the machine and rider are a finely balanced whole, choosing exactly the right speed to hold the right line on every bend, building up enough momentum on each descent to make easy work of the ensuing climb.

▶ Testing steering ◀

First familiarization with the bike should include learning the steering characteristics, and there is no way better than with slow-speed manœuvres. Steering round plastic bottles filled with water is ideal – but don't do this on a public road! The object should be to explore the amount of control you can exert over steering and leaning to perform ever-tighter turns, recover, turn the other way, and so on.

It's quite surprising what the beginner can do after only a short time,

especially on a mountain bike, where the geometry makes for much more forgiving steering than with more upright frames. One word of caution though – unusual muscles will be brought into play as you develop the ability to 'steer from the hips', and their presence will be painfully obvious later in the day, so a hot bath before going to bed is advised.

▶ Testing gears ◀

When you've got to grips with steering and braking, try the gears in earnest. Start at a relatively modest speed – say running pace – just to get used to the feel of the different ratios. Remember, however, not to combine largest chainwheel (outer) with largest cog (inner), or smallest chainwheel (inner) with smallest cog (outer), since that entails too great an offset for the chain to manage without really excessive wear. In practice, there is no great loss, since similarities of ratio are inevitable in an eighteen-gear set, and most manufacturers are clever enough to arrange for the combinations to be either exactly duplicated, or very nearly so.

Although it is interesting for the numerically minded to know what the gear ratios are (see page 63), the proof of the pudding is really in the eating, and a knowledge of what to expect with the thumb-shifters in various positions is the ideal. After a while, most riders subconsciously count their way through the gears, and are soon capable of judging a 'one- or two-click hill', shifting as efficiently as any automatic box on a luxury saloon.

It takes most people a week or so of fairly concentrated riding to get fully familiar with the gears, and the purpose of the initial slow-speed canter while you work the shifters is simply to get used to the fact that pedalling gets harder as the lever on the right is moved towards you, and that on the left is moved away.

Other matters to attend to on your first ride include reaching for the drinking

bottle in its cage (useful practice for one-armed steering), performing road signals, and seeing how steadily the machine can be maintained in a straight line at very low speeds. If you are a beginner, the greatest temptation to overcome in the early stages is taking your feet off the pedals as soon as your brain generates a feeling of insecurity. This will be most marked when you're performing the braking exercises and slow-speed, tight steering. Remember that your balance will alter as your weight becomes redistributed, and the best way to recover from a 'stall' is not to dab the ground with your foot, but to loosen the turn and increase speed by pedalling.

exciting one, for it's only when you get a mountain bike off-road that it really 'comes alive'. The main difference is that the ATB just keeps on going where other bikes give up. This is a function of the extra-low gearing, the broad-treaded tyres, which give extra grip, and a geometry that irons out the minor surface undulations, and follows a fairly consistent line, as long as the rider is determined and firm and keeps up the pressure.

▶ Off-road: points to remember ◀

Use far lower gearing than on the road. It is essential to keep up the momentum no matter what, and a bit of wheel spin as you lose traction from time to time is of no consequence at all (indeed, it tends to act as a kind of limited slip clutch). It's a good idea to get into the smaller chainwheel as soon as the machine leaves the metalled surface, and confine gear-shifting mainly to the rear derailleur, at least until you gain some experience.

Try to keep moving at a constant speed, and anticipate and *avoid* obstacles at first. Negotiating logs and rocks is fairly advanced stuff, and the beginner is better to concentrate on staying on board and getting from A to B on a cross-country course without having to stop, either voluntarily, or because of a lost battle with a particularly hostile piece of environment.

If possible, choose routes which actually go somewhere, and negotiate a variety of different terrain. Your sense of achievement will be greater; and you can repeat the experience, which enables you to measure improvement, and set times to beat.

There is no comparison between the energy you expend on-road, and that which you need to beat across country. Not for nothing is the ATB fitted with a minimum of two bottle cages. Dehydration is a factor on even relatively short rides, and lost moisture must be

▶ FURTHER AFIELD ◀

Most riders will be itching to get off-road, unless they have bought the mountain bike purely for posing. It is as well to enquire where the nearest reasonable rough riding terrain is; in a specialist cycle shop they should know. The legal details of where bicycles can and cannot be ridden are complex, and are covered on pages 100–102.

Initially, off-road riding should be on fairly easy terrain, such as a relatively dry bridleway, so that you can appreciate the difference in the handling characteristics of the machine on rough ground and on tarmac. In the main, the experience will be a rewarding and replaced, or your judgement as well as your stamina will be impaired.

If sightseeing is your object, a moving mountain bike is probably the worst possible platform to choose. Total concentration on the track ahead (if there is one) is required in order to avoid constant spills. There is no disgrace whatever in pausing to admire a view – indeed, it is much of the point of the exercise. Unless a rider gives the trail 100 per cent attention all the time, serious trouble can ensue.

There can be no sensible argument against wearing protective helmets either on- or off-road. True, it is the rider's own decision, and in a free society you are at liberty to live dangerously if you so wish. But the odds against a head injury when you are mountain biking are not high, and it is purely selfish and stupid to worry your friends and relations, not to mention over-burdening an already extended health service, by failing to take the simplest of precautions. Good helmets for mountain biking are light and not hugely expensive, and genuine mountain bikers take their use for granted. Wear one.

There are other useful items of protective clothing. You can get a good solid pair of trainers, or mountain bike shoes if your budget runs that far. Remember to ensure that there are no stray laces to get caught in the transmission. You may think bare legs look good, but see if that compensates for the pain you get riding through a nettle patch! Jogging trousers are OK, but tend to absorb moisture from undergrowth and become soggy. Jeans are worn by many, and were the regulation wear for the early pioneers of mountain biking, but the seams can be very painful over a long distance. Perhaps the best leg-wear is cycling shorts over proper biking tights. Knee pads are useful for really rough ground, although somewhat restricting if worn all the time. Gloves or mitts are a must and towelling wristbands and head-bands can be very useful for keeping sweat out of your eyes. Proper cycling glasses are a must for some routes where midges abound, and some riders feel the need of wind protection for their eyes for all riding.

It is best to build up your strength and experience over relatively easy territory before pitting machine and muscles against really steep gradients. In some parts of the country, of course, this won't be possible, because the easy ground just isn't available. Remember that the mountain bike is designed to be carried if the going gets too tough. Some bikes are equipped with special straps, and other adaptations are possible. Try to get as far up a gradient as possible, getting into the really low gears good and early, and moving out of the saddle to lend weight to the down stroke wherever necessary. (In fact, a lot of rough riding is only possible when you're out of the saddle.)

Descents are the essence of the sport, and downhill is where all the equipment and design of the mountain bike come into their own. For 'hairy' drop-outs and crevasses, lower and extend the saddle rearwards to put as much weight as possible over the rear wheel, for the retarding force of the rear wheel as a drag is essential to downhill control. Slip out of the saddle and assume an even more exaggerated bottom-out posture for the real drop-outs.

In the beginning, it is wise to ride with more experienced mountain bikers on major descents. Watching them will teach you much more than you can learn from a book. Practice is all, and for the sake of both machinery and limbs, don't try to do it all at once. There's no disgrace in taking the slower routes down until you have enough proficiency to pick off the real monsters.

There are a number of excellent mountain biking courses which explain the theory and teach the practical skills, with the help of experienced instructors and well-tried routes. It is a great start for a beginner to acquire a store of mountain biking skills in this way, and then improvise some others over routes which are specially selected for their challenge.

All-terrain riding demands 100 per cent concentration – don't sightsee when riding

First rides and beginners' courses

The Cross-Country Cycling Club is initiating a series of courses for novice off-road riders, including special 'ladies only' sessions, which have been designed to meet demand for the woman rider who wishes to learn the ropes without the pressure of male competition. Contact Geoffrey Apps, 5 Old Station Cottages, Ford, Arundel, West Sussex BN18 0BJ.

The Mountain Bike Club has an established weekend course which covers all aspects of off-road cycling; contact Jeremy Torr, 3 The Shrubbery, Albert Street, Telford, Shropshire TF2 9AS.

The people listed below will also provide a useful first point of contact for the novice off-roader seeking a first ride. They can indicate routes for the more experienced rider as well.

ENGLAND

BEDFORDSHIRE

Mark Cottle
37 Capron Road
Luton
LU4 96U

BERKSHIRE

Tony Silver
31 Lipscombe Close
Newbury
RG14 5JW

BUCKINGHAM-SHIRE

Dave Walker
3 Plumer Road
High Wycombe
HP11 2SS

CLEVELAND

Graham Longstaff
6 Rushmere Heath
Eaglescliffe
Stockton
TS16 9HA

CORNWALL

Andrew Blewett
41 Goonown
St Agnes
TR5 QUY

CUMBRIA

Julian Dyson
5 Duke Street
Gleaston
Ulverston
LA12 0QF

EAST SUSSEX

Nigel Farrow
46 Stafford Road
Brighton
East Sussex

HAMPSHIRE

Mike Carpenter
Aurora
New Inn Road
Bartley
Southampton
SO4 2LR

Steve Rowley
57 Lower Derby Road
Stanshaw
Portsmouth
PO2 8EX

LANCASHIRE

David Flitcroft
19 Brindley Street
Astley Bridge
Bolton
BL1 8QF

GREATER LONDON

Grahame Wallace
109 Church Hill
Cheddington
Leighton Buzzard
Bedfordshire
LU7 OX9

NORFOLK

Johnathan Burt
3 Buck Lane
River Green
Thorpe St Andrew
Norwich

NORTHAMP-TONSHIRE

Sorrell Kinley
Hillside Cottage
Slipton Road
Sudborough
NN14 3BW

NORTHUMBER-LAND

Alan Rainstock
Beaconhill Grange
26 Lockerbie Road
Cramlington
NE23 8DL

OXFORDSHIRE

Ian Wycherley
46 Laburnum Cres
Kidlington
OX5 1HB

SOMERSET

Tim Flooks
St Mary's Court
North Petherton
Bridgwater
TA6 6RA

SOUTH YORKSHIRE

Jake Elliott
64 St Wilfreds Road
Bessacarr
Doncaster
DN4 6AD

SUFFOLK

Tom Sillis
1 Santon House
Santon Downham
IP7 0TT

SURREY

Graeme Peddie
Tanners Hatch YH
Tanners Hatch
Polesden Lacey
Dorking
RH5 68E

Jason Smith
42 Lynwood Gardens
Croydon
CR0 4QH

WEST MIDLANDS

William Dewar
7 Fernwood Croft
Tipton
DY4 8LL

WEST YORKSHIRE

John Stevenson
35 Call Lane
Leeds
LS1 7BT

Stefan Tokarski
25 Glenholme Road
Farsley
Leeds
LS28 5BY

SCOTLAND

BORDERS

Arthur Phillips
Drunmore
Venlaw High Road
Peebles
EH45 8RL

CENTRAL

Chris Bowers
Achabuie
Taynuilt
PA35 1JE

LOTHIAN

Gordon Eady
24 Gilmore Place
Edinburgh
EH3 9NQ

Mike Eawey
c/o Galleon Homes
25 Howe Street
Edinburgh
EH3

WALES

POWYS

Clive Powell
The Mount
East Street
Rhayader
LD6 5DN

Gordon Green
Neuadd Arms Hotel
Llanwryd Wells
LD5 4RT

ENJOYING YOUR SPORT

All mountain bikers have to realize that they are ambassadors for a new and already controversial sport. Unless we behave like diplomats – friendly rather than hostile ones – the sport may be stillborn. It is a fact that powerful lobbies control countryside access. In the main, they would like to restrict that access to feet and hooves. It is not difficult to see why they stongly resist the encroachments of motorized vehicles of any sort, for most countryside enjoyment is enhanced by relative silence. Equally, it is a sad fact that motorcyclists and others have both intimidated and annoyed countryside users with their behaviour and the noise generated by their sport, and laid waste stretches of countryside that they have traversed.

It is vital, if mountain biking is to have a future, that it does not become identified with the already discredited off-road motor-sports in the public mind. This objective is not difficult to achieve with care – after all, the Cyclists' Touring Club, the Rough Stuff Fellowship and the Cross-Country Cycling Club have been unexceptionable countryside users for years. Cyclo-Cross, properly organized and promoted, is an internationally respected sport with a fine history and promising future.

It is true that the beginnings of mountain biking are rooted in a certain non-conformism. In the USA, this unfortunately became rebelliousness and, in certain places, a lack of concern for the safety and convenience of riders and others. This has led to the banning

The Mountain Bike Club
Off-road code

Only ride where you know it is legally OK

Always yield to horses and pedestrians

Avoid animals and crops wherever possible

Take all litter with you

Leave all gates as found

Don't make undue noise

Always be self-sufficient, both for yourself and your bike

Never create any sort of fire hazard

Avoid bunching up and obstructing a trail when riding in a group

Always tell someone where you are going

Be pleasant to other countryside users – getting angry never solves a problem

of bikes from many trails in a number of states. NORBA, the national association in the USA, has its work cut out trying to overcome the thoughtlessness of those early beginnings. It is vital that the same short-sightedness does not mar the development of the sport in the UK and Europe. Britain is small in territory, but has much to be proud of, in both the extent and the rich variety of its countryside. The demands upon that countryside, and the conditions which attend them, are complex. If people who have satisfied those demands and conditions are to admit another group of users to their midst, they need to be satisfied that they will be endangering neither the countryside itself not their own enjoyment.

In the USA, and to an extent in Europe as well, it is being suggested that the tyres of mountain bikes undercut the surface of softer terrain, leading to soil erosion, and that access should therefore be restricted, or denied altogether. Such an argument is – in the main – spurious. True, it is possible to create damage by gross misuse of mountain bikes, skidding and sliding and so on, but these techniques are anyway neither necessary nor safe for touring cross-country. They are valid competitive techniques, but are then restricted to courses specifically obtained for the purpose, with appropriate agreements from the correct authorities, landowners and users. Mountan bikes, correctly used, create less damage than horses to the trail. They pose far less danger to other trail and path users, and little or no hazard to other road users on the metalled roads leading to, or interconnecting, off-road routes.

The ATB machines themselves are

completely benign. Riders can be a different proposition. The people most likely to be inconvenienced by mountain bikes, and therefore most likely to pose a threat to the sport, are ramblers, horse riders and other users of paths and trails where cycle access is legal. It is therefore absolutely vital to respect their pastime and not intimidate them or compromise their enjoyment in any way.

Of course, there will be those who just do not wish to see any increase in usership of territory they have come to regard as their own, and their protests can be strident, even when every courtesy towards them has been observed. Even then, it is vital, if mountain biking is to be recognized as an accepted countryside sport, that the biker's behaviour should be exemplary. Do not respond to abuse; don't argue. Give a polite 'Sorry you see it that way' and ride away; you will never win an argument with such a person, and you must deny them the satisfaction of any complaint against you.

▶ LEGAL ACCESS ◀

The law regarding bicycles off-road is complex and unclear, and only a summary of it can be given here. *Bicycle Action* magazine, in association with the CTC (Cycle Tourists' Association), have produced an excellent little booklet entitled *Cycling Off-road and the Law*, and this can be obtained from the CTC for £1.25.

Generally speaking, *bridleways* are open to cyclists, provided they give way to walkers and horse riders. This right can be varied by local authorities, but they must post suitable traffic signs ('No Cycling').

The position is far less clear with *footpaths*. The law does not specifically prohibit the riding of cycles on footpaths, although 'carriages' are prohibited. A cycle is a 'carriage' within the meaning of the 1980 Highway Act, so technically riding on a footpath is illegal. No case has yet come to court to

test the law, but it is only common sense to assume that if one did, prosecution would be strongly supported by ramblers and other groups, so it is in the interests of cyclists to avoid such a case. The law even extends to wheeling bicycles along footpaths, while the cyclist is temporarily dismounted, say between bridleways on a cross-country ride. So make sure you don't push cycles in such a way as to make it difficult for others to pass.

Footways are a different name for pavements. It is always an offence to ride on them.

Roads used as public paths (RUPPs) are similar in law to bridleways. However, there is a process of re-definition going on, and although the tendency is to assume that they were once bridleways, and therefore open to cycling, there is an outside chance that some may be downgraded to footpaths. If in doubt, check with the relevant highway authority.

Unclassified country roads (UCRs) are open to cycling.

Canal towpaths, while not specifically open to cyclists, may be classified as bridleways, and therefore accessible, or cyclists may need to be allocated a permit by the British Waterways Board. In most cases, it is specifically prohibited to cycle through locks, and riders should either dismount and walk or avail themselves of the handy little bypasses provided by the more thoughtful authorities, such as Thames Conservancy.

Forest tracks were once very restricted, but increasingly forest rides are becoming available, and some with the mountain biker very much in mind. This is also the case with some of our bigger *reservoirs*, such as Rutland Water, where every facility – including bike hire, refreshment and picnic points and a host of other enlightened features – is provided and regularly maintained. This is a prime example of the sort of treatment mountain biking can expect if its supporters and adherents show themselves to be responsible and caring countryside users.

Rutland Water – an area of natural beauty which welcomes mountain bikers

The decline in agricultural use of land is confronting landowners with the dilemma of how to preserve the countryside from development, yet still earn enough to maintain a viable operation. This means that those of us who wish to enjoy the recreation of the countryside must be prepared to pay for what might hitherto have been free, if we are to avoid the ultimate horror of having nothing to cycle through but endless suburbs. The sport itself has much to contribute towards encouraging this trend: where a good route exists, we can work with landowners, other potential users and local authority recreation departments to help bring about multi-user facilities. Individual clubs can do much to help in this respect, providing expertise for routing, helping to develop useful local codes of conduct for the facility, and working to establish mutual understanding and good relations with other users.

▶ THE ADVANCED STUFF ◀

Before we get to the hard information, it is necessary to preface this chapter with a few words about the objective of mountain biking.

Sure, you can ride a mountain bike just like a dirt-track motorcycle, executing flat-out slides with one foot trailing, and shifting a large part of the environment as you go. You might have a lot of fun. Of course, you might also hurt yourself, or someone else, and if you habitually perform these manœuvres in some place where people go to enjoy other, quieter country pursuits, you will undoubtedly harden opposition to mountain biking.

If enough people use mountain bikes to carve up the countryside and other people's enjoyment of it , this book may end up having mere historical value. Good mountain bikers are those who value and respect the environment, and try to leave it as they found it. The same constraints apply to horse riders. They can, with a little practice, jump five-bar gates and gallop at breakneck speed across uneven country, but you don't see them doing it outside properly controlled events and point-to-points. Mountain biking is no different. It requires skills which, when learned, are exhilarating (and sometimes life-preserving), but which need to be practised in the right place at the right time.

Mountain biking is a great way of seeing more of the wild places than you can possibly reach by motorized transport, and more of them than would be accessible in the same time on foot. It is a properly organized sport – although still in its infancy – and it is an athletic skill. The purpose of this section is to introduce the keen rider to the advanced skills required to maintain mastery of the machine and the body over difficult ground. It's up to each individual rider to have enough self-control to know when *not* to behave like a real gonzo!

▶ PUSHING OUT THE LIMITS ◀

While new riders should get themselves off-road as soon as possible, it is recommended that they leave the more extreme and adventurous manœuvres until they have acquired sufficient skill and confidence with basic riding. You also need to build up your stamina and endurance, and develop the muscles brought into play by extended off-road riding to the point where they no longer ache at the end of every trip. Fitness is very important to the mountain biker. It's inevitable that you will have falls and upsets – with monotonous frequency at the beginning, lessening as time goes by – and the fit rider has a great advantage when it comes both to sustaining less injury from a fall, and to recovering quickly from what effects the injury does have.

In 'How to Ride 1', one suggestion was practising tight turns and braking distances round plastic water-filled bottles on tarmac; the same technique is a very good way of finding you how the bike behaves on different surfaces. It will also help you to establish the tyre pressures which give the best results on different types of terrain. In the UK, unlike sunny southern California, mud, rather than dry sandy soils, will be a constant feature. Reducing tyre pressure – more in the rear wheel than the front, as that is where you need optimum traction – is a big help. The actual pressure will vary according to the terrain and your weight. For a lightish rider floundering around in mud, without too many hidden hard bits like rocks, 15 lbs/sq.in is about as low as you can afford to go, bearing in mind that the terrain over which you travel is constantly changing, and you don't want to be forever pumping up and deflating tyres.

One of the great advantages of the mountain bike is this ability to increase traction by reducing the pressure in big 'knobblies'. But it does none the less have its limitations, and it is well to be aware of them from the outset. The most serious problem is that a very low-

pressure tyre will lose most of its shock-absorbing properties, and will no longer bounce over small, sharp bits of rock. This will increase the risk of punctures through compression damage to the inner tube as it is crimped against the rim. Have a very well-equipped puncture outfit with you at all times – and carrying a spare tube is no bad idea. Rim damage can result from too hard a bash against too big a rock. You'll know when this happens: a juddering shock is transmitted through the frame, and the noise is fairly distinctive! This is one of the reasons why the pressure should never be reduced so drastically in the front tyre. Unless something very odd is happening, the front wheel will hit most obstacles first, and the shock absorbency of the tyre is essential in preventing the machine from stopping rather faster than the rider, with the inevitable outcome.

You can minimize the potential for rear wheel rim damage by spending quite a lot of time out of the saddle when negotiating rocky ground. This allows greater control anyway but it also reduces the weight over the back wheel and is good for tyres, inner-tubes, rims and spines!

Watch out for 'tyre-creep' when you under-inflate tyres. The effect of tyre-creep is to pull at the inner tube, often so severely as to damge the valve joint, causing anything from a slow puncture – which is unnoticeable for a while – to a blowout – which is usually obvious even to the least sensitive of riders! It happens because the bead is no longer held so tightly against the rim by the pressure of the tube, and because of the often explosive effects of pedalling to overcome gradients and obstacles. The increased adhesion of the under-inflated tyre also plays a part in it. The

cure is to coat the inside of the tyre and the rim itself with a rubber cement – Cow Gum is OK, as long as you let it dry before re-fitting tyre and tube. These adhesives never really dry out, so they do a good job of holding everything still, whilst still permitting tube removal.

A pump is not fitted to every new mountain bike, and there are riders who like to remove every accessory that doesn't actually contribute to forward motion. This is plainly unwise when you are riding off-road, since even if you do escape punctures, you will still need a pump to deflate, then re-flate, tyres. It's wrong to rely on other riders if you're travelling in a group; outdoor sports, especially the riskier ones, demand self-sufficiency. It makes sense to cover all conceivable risks.

One very good answer to the pump problem is a sturdy and well-engineered seat pin which converts into a pump. This US import, supplied by Madison Freewheel, exemplifies the inspired design thinking now emanating from the US, and re-volutionizing ATB equipment, even as this book is written.

The question of mudguards is one to decide for yourself. There are very adequate ATB mudguards available, and in soggy going they are a boon, preventing a vast amount of mire collecting on you and others in your group. In fact, it's dangerous to travel too close behind another bike in wet and rough going if it has no mud-guards, because a soft knobbly tyre can pick up small stones and bits of mud, and throw them some distance. On the other hand, with really rough going in very sticky conditions, the guards can clog up and be more of a menace than a help. The best solution is to have mudguards, but be prepared to dis-pense with them if a particular run looks as it it will make them a hindrance.

This last point emphasizes the need for sensible pre-planning of all but the shortest, most casual off-road excur-sions. Good riders should never be caught out by the conditions, or even worse, by their equipment. If you're inexperienced, stick to routes you know well in the beginning, or to routes which are well documented in moun-tain bike literature, such as those described on pages 114–31. Always take tools, vital spares, maps and – if you're really getting off the beaten track – a compass.

To be proficient, the mountain biker has to have mastered three main skill areas in addition to the normal riding skills: **climbing**, **descending** and **avoi-dance**. They are distinct disciplines in themselves, and as such tend to be recognized in the organized aspects of the sport. Each appears as a separate event in mountain bike rallies, under the guise of hillclimb, downhill slalom and observed trial. A cross-country race will merge all the skills over mixed terrain, at speed, and with a whole lot

The seatpin pump – clever US innovation marries a sturdy seatpin with an efficient inflator

of other people all coveting the same six square inches of mud at precisely the same time. It is quite interesting.

Each of these techniques will present different problems according to the sur-face on which it is performed, and the prevailing condition of the going – wet, dry, frozen, compacted or chopped-up. It is only possible in the context of a book to outline the athletic and skill requirements of each of the disciplines in broad terms. You must apply practice and experience to a variety of conditions to really be a master of all types of going, and you never really stop learn-ing. Other variables will come from your equipment, since differing frame designs, variable wheel sizes and alter-nating rider positions will all have an effect on performance. Your bike might be a good climber, but a slightly twitchy descender, or it might have a host of other characteristics. These will all affect your execution of new techniques.

about mountain biking which tends to separate it from other cycling: climbing means *getting to the top*. No matter if the going is so tough that you even have to carry the wretched machine halfway, you get to the top, because the whole point of the exercise is going down again!

The most successful climbers have developed techniques for getting as far up a steep incline as possible. Sit high up, with the seat pin on the maximum comfortable extension and the saddle forward of the normal position and far forward of the descent position. Adopt a less crouched, straighter posture than for normal riding, and be prepared to pull on those handlebars to get the maximum power into the pedals.

Start off in low gears, rather than selecting them as the gear you're pushing becomes too hard. On all but the latest Shimano XT front and rear derailleurs, you are asking for trouble changing under pressure. (But the top of the Shimano ATB range changers seem to thrive on pressure changes, and as a result are becoming standard-fit on more of the serious machinery.)

Regardless of the changers, low gear spinning with the highest cadence possible is the key to the early stages of any hill, and the elliptical Biopace-type chainring is regarded by some as a further must for serious climbing. Get those pedals turning fast, and steer round rough patches wherever practical. It will not always be possible to manage the ascent from the saddle. Standing on the pedals and moving the bike from side to side (known as 'honking') is the way to stamp out the particularly steep bits, and lost traction can result from this unless you really 'hang your tail out' to transfer weight over the rear end.

This can all be very tiring, so vary the technique – from seated 'spinning', working hard in the saddle to keep the pedal rate up, to standing and 'honking' up the hill. You can also get wheelspin when you climb seated, because you are further forward over the bottom-bracket

▶ *Climbing* ◀

It has been said that it's not a whole lot of good having a mountain bike if you don't climb with it! We would take issue with that statement, since one of the inherent features of the ATB is its great safety, which makes it a good all-round choice for even fen dwellers, if they want to get off-road. The fact remains, however, that climbing is inbred into the mountain bike, and mastery of the steep bits is necessary if you want to be regarded as an aficionado.

The problems associated with climbing – assuming that the rider is reasonably fit – have to do with finding a sustainable cadence (pedalling rate), achieving traction on a variable surface, and maintaining enough speed to make the machine controllable. A rider may also be confronted with various obstacles, some of which just cannot be ridden.

At once let us accept a basic truth

than when you're more crouched.
Again, you overcome this by standing
and shifting your weight rearwards.

Watch any group of experienced riders, and note the amount of time they
spend out of the saddle. For mountain
bikers it is much longer than for ordinary cyclists; the stance holds them
poised for instant shifts of balance and
transfers of weight to cope with ever-
changing gradient and terrain, and with
the lightening effect on the front wheel
which, if it's not corrected by bending
the arms to bring weight forward again,
can lift them off-course and cause them
to topple sideways.

As a rule of thumb, you're better off
in a slightly higher gear for 'honking' or
standing climbing than for seated spinning. If you're going for a varied
approach – and that's the most efficient
one – then it is inevitable that your gears
are going to get changed under relative
pressure. The serious off-road rider will
never economize on the gears for that
very reason. The problem can be solved
by intelligent technique. Even on the
steepest hill, there will be sections
where you can momentarily ease the
pressure to change up, and then get up
on those pedals and pump some iron
for thirty or forty yards, using the
added momentum you've gained to
ease off fractionally again and come
down a gear for a spell in the saddle.

Try to take the less broken patches of
ground seated, saving the greater control – but greater effort – of the standing
posture for the more grotty bits.

It cannot be repeated often enough
that these descriptions can only be
broad advice. The conditions change so
much from ride to ride, and a shale- and
slate-strewn Welsh mountain will differ
fundamentally from an ascent of a muddy gully in the Chilterns. The only sure
way is practice, and a firm belief in
improvisation.

Aids to performance for hill climbing
will certainly include toe-clips and
straps, because they help really drag
those pedals round; and a stem–bar
combination that does not groan alar-
mingly as do some aluminium to

aluminium combos when they are really being stressed. (They may not actually be at risk, but it doesn't help your morale to think the bars could snap off at any moment!) And get a really sound front and rear derailleur system. The front changer may not be called on to do much, but if the bike is attacking a ridge which goes down as well as up several times in its length, then the smaller chainwheel will have to be out of the picture for some of the time at least. All but the very best front changers flunk the job of pressure shifting, and it is just not worth fitting them to a real 'mountain goat'. Biopace or equivalent chainrings are practically standard on most serious mountain bikes now. The scientific arguments in their favour are very complex; simpler fare is the opinion of those who have tried both round and oval in the mountains, and most seem to favour the oval rings. They certainly look right – and feeling good about one's kit is worth at least another hundred yards on any climb...

▶ Descending ◀

The proverb runs: 'That which goes up, must come down' – certainly true of mountain bikes. And, if possible, the mountain biker should come down at around the same time, roughly on top of the machine. Here's how it's done (sometimes).

Braking is critical. You are constantly compensating for the machine's natural inclination to hurtle down the slope at 32 ft per second (squared). You do this by using the rear brake as a drag for part of the time; the rear brake is a safer decelerator in the downhill mode than the front brake on a machine where the front loading is now far too acute. However, the back brake will be ineffective if it is used alone, so, wherever possible, on the straight bits, gently apply the front cantilevers as well to give the rear brakes some assistance, and scrub off more speed.

At the same time, you must overcome that imbalance towards the front end, and the most effective way of achieving

that is to lower the saddle right down, and stick your bottom out as far as possible, with your arms extended, and thighs gripping the sides of the saddle. Many mountain bikes are fitted with rear panniers, not to carry luggage, but to prevent some extemporary and rather painful surgery being inflicted by a rapidly revolving, very knobbly rear tyre. You have been warned. Such a posture certainly increases the effectiveness of the rear brake by transferring more weight to the back wheel, but a descent will vary in grade and severity as well, and there will be times when the 'technical' nature of the ground will require more delicacy than blasting down, bum trailing, trusting all to a near burnt-out set of brake blocks!

When you near a section where you have to pick your way through rocks or other obstacles, increase braking pressure on both brakes until the speed is brought more under control, and come forward in the saddle gently, getting the pedals level to give maximum ground

The pannier – a touring necessity

Following contours on a very sharp descent

clearance on both sides. You can attempt the terrain seated or standing, depending on how much control you require to haul the bike round, over and through various obstructions. One of the more profound observations about mountain bike descents points out that 'You only really get it all together for seconds at a time' but it fails to explain the depth of panic that makes up the spaces in between those sublime seconds!

Straight down is not always the best way. Only an experienced (another word for scarred) rider will recognize the gentle understatement in that proposition. On impossibly steep slopes, a zig-zag technique akin to true slalom skiing is employed. The rider follows the contours of the slope, rather than the slope itself, taking a switchback route down. To go from zig to zag, use a false turn into the slope to give the fast lean which will change direction quickest. This technique takes some practising, and it's important to achieve a fairly shallow contouring, so your turn speed is not too great, as a tumble on such

extreme slopes can go on for some time.

A variant on the false turn, to be tried only by very experienced riders, and practised initially on gentle slopes with a forgiving surface, is a turn produced by applying the front brake and simultaneously leaning forward in order to lift·the rear wheel, and so commence the action referred to affectionately as a 'face plant'. As the rear wheel starts to rise, shift your body weight in the direction of the turn, and the back of the machine will start to come round. At this point you have to lean in the opposite direction to maintain balance, slackening front brake pressure when the machine faces in the general direction required. The rear wheel will return to earth fairly forcibly and it's a pretty good idea to straighten up the bars around now. This is not a recommended high-speed, high-altitude manœuvre for any but the most skilled.

Getting to the stage where a stunt of the calibre of the above can be safely accomplished will mean plenty of jumping and hopping practice before you venture to where the oxygen is rare, sanity rarer.

In fact, lifting the front wheel over obstructions and out of gullies ('popping a wheelie' in the vernacular) and pulling up the rear wheel after it ('bunnyhopping') are valid and useful techniques, and not just stunts. If you're confronted by a six-inch rock step on a fastish descent over treacherous going, your choices are stark. You can attempt to stop, which usually involves a sideslip and a (relatively) controlled fall, if there's room. You can pile straight into the obstruction, risking front forks and wheel rim, and testing helmet to destruction. Or you can hop over the problem.

Throw your body weight right back, at the same time pulling hard on the bars to get the front wheel airborne. The pull-back action should coincide with adopting a standing position if you're not already in it, so that you can flex your knees to absorb the shock of the rear wheel hitting the obstacle, and transfer your weight forward over the bottom-bracket again to prevent the wheelie going over too far (very unlikely, fortunately).

If you combine that with a bunnyhop to get the rear wheel over the obstruction, you are really doing the business, and also protecting rear rim and tyre from impact damage. And it really only leaves the problem of a safe two-point landing, much of which will depend on the surface the bike touches down upon. To get that rear wheel up, transfer weight forward hard immediately the front wheel is in the air and over the obstacle. This will force the front wheel back down and, if executed with enough force, lift off the back to get it over too. Push hard on the pedals to drive the bike over the step as soon as the rear wheel touches down; most riders under- rather than overdo this manoeuvre, and the rear end will need further help to clear fully.

Wheelies and hops, and timing the power strokes to force the bike to follow through its own momentum over obstacles, are at the heart of good cross-country riding, and it's a good idea to lay out a course on rough but fairly level ground for practice. If a group of riders do this regularly together, they can coach each other and learn from each other's strong points. Remember, 100 yards down from the summit of a Welsh slate quarry, going like the clappers, is not the ideal place to debut that classy stunt you just read about!

Variations on wheelies and hops include introducing a sideways shift into the movement to sidestep out of gullies and other such hazards. This can also be accomplished with enough speed by just riding out of the ditch, but the machine will tend to sideslip back in, and you must be ready to fight it out with the ensuing skid by turning briefly into the direction of the slip to get back upright, re-establish control and have another go.

Sideslipping can be induced by turning the bars away from the direction of intended travel and applying rear brake, trailing a foot in the direction of lean, rather like a speedway rider. Spectacular as this stunt appears, it is *not* good mountain biking practice, save for out-and-out racing. It chops up loose surfaces very badly and should really be kept as a reserve technique to minimize the danger of head-on impacts with large obstacles or to overcome too fast an entry to a bend.

Once you gain a modicum of proficiency, the overwhelming feeling is one of confidence in the seemingly unbeatable characteristics of the bike. ATBs are real scrappers and, in the right hands, can perform some pretty impressive feats. Don't ever take this for granted, though. Relax for a second, and the terrain will catch bike and rider out. The ability constantly to shift balance, the concentration to pick the line of least resistance on any descent, an absolute knowledge of braking distances and performance over all types of going, athleticism and sheer nerve are all essential for advanced riding.

Once a rider has acquired enough skill to be safe on the rougher terrain, the urge to stray further afield than the local bridleways will become overwhelming.

Even at this stage, the sensible mountain biker will be seeking to improve riding ability, and this will be a good time to invest in one of the courses which are springing up around the country to teach safe and skilful riding. A course can be a couple of days over a weekend, or a more ambitious week-long affair in the Welsh mountains, or at an increasing number of holiday/training centres. A far from comprehensive list appears on page 95; if you can find nothing convenient for you, contact the Mountain Bike Club, who run their own training in Telford, Shropshire, and who are in the know about other training. Another excellent source of information is the Cross Country Cycling Club, whose regular magazine, *Making Tracks*, is a superb information exchange for adventurous cyclists everywhere on matters technical, forthcoming events, training and social rides, competition and routes.

We are indebted to the Cross Country Cycling Club for the material in this section, which is a series of routes, reproduced from their pages. The mountain biker is constantly on the lookout for routes and rides, particularly as access is by no means easy in some parts of the country. *Making Tracks* encourages riders to send in their own favourite routes, and these maps and instructions are perfect examples of how to prepare succinct, useful navigation instructions for mountain biking.

The development of the recreational side of the sport depends to a great extent on all participants contributing information of this sort, *but* if you are publicizing a route, be sure to check with local authorities and landowners that legal access does exist, otherwise you risk damaging the sport's image.

Finally, remember to stay within the mountain bike code (page 98) at all times when cycling off-road, especially when crossing private land. Cyclists and horse riders are often dependent on the goodwill of landowners for access, and even when a right of way exists, bad behaviour on the part of users can lead to obstruction from landowners; the ensuing fuss is inconvenient to everybody.

The routes in this section are not intended to be a comprehensive guide to mountain biking across the UK. That would take a book on its own. These routes show the types of riding available to enthusiasts, and signpost one of the other great joys of mountain biking – ferreting out new routes, and plotting and documenting them for others.

The following directory is intended as a basic research file, from which the keen mountain biker can build up a dossier of routes around the country.

It is the responsibility of individual riders to ensure in advance, by checking with landowners and local authorities, that they are not breaking the law when they ride cross-country.

Location
North York Moors National Park
Farndale Circular

Start
Ingleby Greenhowe 582064
(nearest station Battersby
Junction)

Distance
overall   33.6 km/21 miles
road   6.4 km/4 miles
rough   27.2 km/17 miles
Full day trip with pub lunch stop

Terrain
Open heather moorland with small
amount of plantation. Easy going
after hard climbs

Going
Old roads, dismantled railway lines,
estate tracks, open moorland which
can be soft in parts. Good condition
all year round

Maps
North York Moors tourist map
O.S. Landranger sheets 94 and 93
O.S. Outdoor Leisure 26

The North York Moors are an isolated upland area surrounded by the Tees Valley to the North, the Vale of Pickering to the South, the North Sea to the East and the Vale of York to the West. The moors rise to a maximum of 1490 feet at Botton Head and the area boasts the largest open tract of heather moorland in the country, around 160 square miles.

The area is ideal for mountain biking, for once the initial climb to the top is behind, then there are miles upon miles of flat open moorland crisscrossed with old drove roads, bridleways, estate roads and dismantled railway lines. The valleys are steep-sided, giving exciting descents and lung-bursting climbs.

This route is a circular tour over the high moor to the beautiful valley of Farndale, starting and finishing at the village of Ingleby Greenhowe, famous for its local hostelry, the Dudley Arms. Ingleby also has a beautiful Norman church, and the village nestles below the Cleveland Hills or 'Cliff Land' as the Vikings used to call them.

If travelling by car, use the large Dudley Arms car park at the road junction in the village. Train travellers can take the Esk Valley line from Middlesborough, getting off at Battersby Halt, which is 2 miles from Ingleby.

Ignore the Dudley (that pleasure awaits your return), and set off towards Battersby, turning right at the top of the hill, signposted Bank Foot, keeping straight on at the Hamlet towards Ingleby Forest. The closed forestry gate marks the start of the climb up Turkey Nab using the old public highway between Stokesley and Kirby Moorside. Halfway up the hill there is another gate which allows a justifiable rest before continuing the climb. Patches of old tarmacadam confirm that the road was once in better condition but beyond the gate the surface deteriorates with a lot of loose fist-sized stones. After a rocky step the road turns sharp right and the grassy bridleway branching off to the left is now taken, leaving the loose surface behind.

Stopping at this point to catch your breath enables you to enjoy the view across to Easby Moor with its monument to Captain Cook; beyond lies Roseberry Topping and further on still the industrial heartland of Teesside.

After resting continue upwards on the grassy track towards the skyline and, crossing a plank bridge, keep straight on, ignoring the track off to the right. A deep drainage ditch has to be negotiated before reaching the Cleveland Way track marked with a small cairn.

Go straight across, taking a well-maintained track over the open moorland descending to the bridge over Black Beck and up and over the ridge descending to join the flagged track, probably an old pack-horse route to Baysdale Abbey. Don't get too carried away on this track because after a short distance a large cairn on your right marks the bridleway to Burton Howe which climbs steadily across the moor, on a track that can be heavy after rain, to the Bronze Age burial mound of Burton Howe.

Upon arrival at the Howe take another rest and enjoy the view across the valley to the impressive northern escarpment of the North York Moors. Whilst enjoying this view try to imagine that during the Bronze Age the Moors were forested and that the burial mound would have been located in a forest clearing. The heather moorland that now surrounds you is entirely man-made and is maintained to support the sport of grouse shooting.

Rejoin the old Stokesley to Kirby Moorside road just beyond the Howe and turn left (south) towards Bloworth Crossing and Rutland Rigg. At the old railway crossing at Bloworth, which marks the junction with the Lyke Wake Walk, continue south with views of Bransdale on the right. Don't rush along this track because the views are superb and the old road is marked with old crosses and standing stones.

After two miles there is a crossroads of tracks at Ousegill Head where you must turn left on to another old road which descends Monket Bank into Farndale. Take care on the descent because there are a number of drainage gulleys crossing the track which can cause problems. This track demands concentration as the surface deteriorates and the gradient steepens, and when you finally stop at the gate and look across Farndale, bear in mind that there were once plans to build a reservoir and flood this valley.

At the gate turn right and then left again, taking the road to the Feversham Arms in Church Houses for a welcome pint and a bar meal. In springtime the bikes can be left at the pub and a pleasant walk alongside the River Dove, to view the famous daffodils, can be enjoyed.

After refuelling turn right upon leaving the pub and then immediately left towards Castleton. This is the start of a long hard climb, on tarmac, to Blakey Junction, where the old Rosedale Ironstone railway line used to pass under the main road. You can still see part of the old bridge. If further refreshment is required then turn left along the road to the Lion at Blakey, if this temptation can be resisted then take the old railway west, back to Bloworth Crossing. Before setting off, cross the road and look across the valley of Rosedale where you can see the old ironstone workings and the old railway contouring around the valley. If you want to extend this ride, by about 8 miles, then it is possible to ride the old railway around Rosedale, returning to Blakey before setting off for Bloworth. The railway contours around Farndale and there are good views into Westerdale from the embankment above Esklets. The surface of the old railway is excellent but it is exposed and can be hard work with a headwind.

At Bloworth go straight on and follow the old railway to the top of the three-quarter-mile long Ingleby incline, where wagons used to be hauled up to the railhead on the moor top. It is not wise to throw caution to the wind and swoop down the incline unless you can bunny-hop the locked gate halfway down. If you are in control look out for a crude carving of a man in a stove-pipe hat in the rock on the right-hand side of the second cutting, which was probably made by the navvies who worked on the construction of the incline. After the gate you can now safely release the brakes and enjoy an exhilarating descent to the cinder track that bears right at the bottom to a locked forestry gate. At the gate it can be appreciated why the route should be ridden in a clockwise direction – an anti-clockwise route would mean climbing the incline.

The old railway continues through a gate and past some Forestry Commission cottages on an excellent track that is a gradual downhill gradient back to Bank Foot, from where you can retrace your tyre tracks back to Ingleby and, if your timing is right (6 p.m. opening), a final beer at the Dudley Arms before going home.

Graham Longstaff

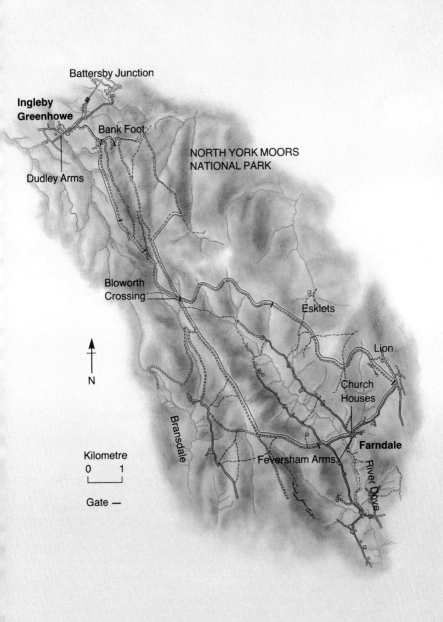

Battersby Junction

Ingleby
Greenhowe

Bank Foot

Dudley Arms

NORTH YORK MOORS
NATIONAL PARK

Bloworth
Crossing

Esklets

Lion

N

Church
Houses

Bransdale

Farndale

Kilometre
0   1

River Dove

Gate —

Feversham Arms

Location
Forest of Bowland, Lancashire

Start
Dunsop Bridge

Distance (approximate)
overall 24 km/15 miles
road   5 km/3 miles
rough   19 km/12 miles

Terrain
Demanding but with superb views,
valley track and high moor; no
woodland

Going
Surfaced access tracks, hill paths
and open moorland, boggy in places
– compass recommended

Maps
O.S. Landranger sheet 103

Start the ride at Dunsop Bridge, a small village at the confluence of the River Dunsop and River Hodder. The 'Thorneyholme Hotel' the far bank of the River Hodder is very nice and provides tea and scones at a reasonable price.

From Dunsop Bridge follow the road sign for the Trough of Bowland. This is a minor road passing a primary school to the right; the road in unfenced and sheep are in abundance, as are cattle grids – no problem.

The road follows the trough along the course of Langden Beck, a pleasant stream – continue past two left turns (into Water Board Property).

Pass a farm which spans the road and continue until you see a small barn on your right; next to this is a gate – the track is not signposted – through the gate and up the very rough stony track, which climbs the hill and skirts a small mixed-tree plantation; follow this track through a small ruin to the point where it degenerates into rough pasture.

At this point, look up the hill to the east (compass!) and you can see, just, a stile – head towards it and, at the top, you are on a peat plateau called Whin Fell (476m).

Check your bearings/OS map and cross the plateau; navigation is made easy by yellow toppped posts, which are sensibly placed – just far enough apart, if your map reading is lacking, you won't get lost, but not so obvious you lose the feeling of remoteness.

Here, on the tops, beware of peat hags (which will swallow your front wheel given half a chance); pick the right time of year and the top is covered with cotton grass in bloom.

As you reach the far side of the top, you get a breathtaking view across the valley of the Brennand River to Middle Knoll, a dome-shaped hill (395m). The path to take down this far side of Whin Fell is obvious and precarious, where the path has been washed away in scree; you may have to carry your bike for the first hundred yards or so – it is on the side of a very steep slope.

In the bottom of the valley, near Brennand Farm, you come back on to a farm road. After the first steep section, the descent is sublime, and all rideable. You have a choice: take the easy route on your right, down and around Middle Knoll, anti-clockwise, or take the more difficult and rewarding track on the left – through the farm – nice people – and up a steep rocky landrover track across a saddle between Middle Knoll and Brennand Fell. The track graduates to moorland at the summit, but pathfinding is easy.

Go over the crest of the hill and you will see a small community of houses; Whitendale, situated on the Whitendale River. The descent is interesting; it starts gently and gets more and more steep as you go down, made all the more interesting, as at the bottom there is no run off; only a drop into the River.

Cross the river – using the footbridge is advisable (but perhaps slightly less exciting) – and go left through a gate past the houses. Follow the track across pasture and, at the point where it changes to moorland, identify a gap in the coniferous plantation due north, and head for that.

Beyond the plantation, take the path which follows Whitendale River for approximately one mile. At the crossing of the second side tributary on the right, head up the hill north-east up Hard Hill Top – you'll probably be pushing by now – about halfway up, you'll come across a track following the contour of this hill.

Here, turn right and follow the track south-east across Croasdale Fell – this is pleasantly rideable.

The track turns into a road after approximately 4.5 km, at which point, depending on how you feel, you can follow the lanes, which are pleasant and quiet, wander your way to Slaidburn for a pint and

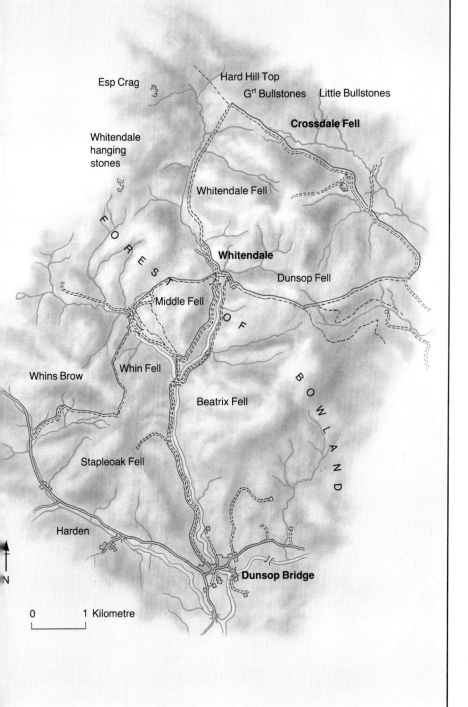

Esp Crag

Hard Hill Top

Gʳᵗ Bullstones   Little Bullstones

Crossdale Fell

Whitendale
hanging
stones

Whitendale Fell

F
O
R
E
S
T

Whitendale

Dunsop Fell

Middle Fell

O
F

Whins Brow

Whin Fell

B
O
W
L
A
N
D

Beatrix Fell

Stapleoak Fell

Harden

Dunsop Bridge

N

0   1 Kilometre

on to Dunsop Bridge, or you can follow the bridleway on your right, which leads west across the width of Dunsop Fell.

This route is rideable and culminates in a (tricky in parts) descent, back into Whitendale.

Now for the final part of the ride: check how your legs feel. Can they stand a bit more off-road? If so, take the track on the east bank of Whitendale River and follow it downstream to the confluence of Whitendale and Brennand Rivers which together make the River Dunsop. Then cross the bridge and back on to a track, which is made-up and belongs to the North West Water Authority. Back into Dunsop Bridge.

If you've had enough after the descent of Dunsop Fell, continue back into Whitendale and take the made-up road, which follows the contour of Middle Knoll and later joins the NWWA track.

This area of England is generally bypassed by your average daytripper, who prefers to head for the crowded Lake District. Whilst the Trough of Bowland area may not offer as much as the Lakes in dramatic scenery, it is a lot quieter, even on bank holidays and weekends, and offers cross-country riding challenges to compare with anywhere in Our Fair Country.

Dave Flitcroft

Location
North Downs, Surrey

Start
Westcott village green (train to Dorking and ride to Westcott)
Alternative Starts Gomshall or Dorking Town station, or Holmbury St Mary YH

Distance
overall 19 km/12 miles
road   4 km/2.5 miles
rough   15 km/9.5 miles

Terrain
Undulating chalk and sandstone wooded hills

Going
Deep water throughout the year — to be avoided

Maps
O.S. Landranger sheet 187
O.S. Pathfinder sheets TQ 40/41

(Although the majority of the off-road sections are bridleways, some are footpaths. We therefore suggest that riders use their discretion as to how they use these sections.)

Being situated in the south-east, this ride will appear deceptively easy to those for whom elevation is all in terms of achievement in cross-country cycling. Nevertheless, in the summer or frosty months it makes a most pleasant day jaunt for those who aren't mud fanciers. Although you are never far from

civilization, it is wise to carry some survival kit, especially in Winter.

Find your way to Westcott village green, by whatever means you may, and head west towards the Cricketers pub and take the lane that runs uphill of the main A25. Pass the church on your right and take the next lane on the right. Follow this until the lane veers sharp right, but at this point dive into the woods straight ahead for a little sandy (and cautious) yomping down to the A25 again. That was simply a 100% better way of getting half a mile down the main road. Now turn sharp left into the drive/track to Rookery Hill Farm. Follow this through until it becomes a normal-type bridleway contouring up the side of a small valley. Straight ahead you'll see a footpath leading up to the right but ignore this and veer to the left, following the path until it enters the woods. At this point you have the first, and probably the biggest, challenging hill of the day, so get you trials hat on and plug on up that hill.

At the top, turn left to join a broad track that runs the ridge. Stay more or less on the edge of the wood, picking the most suitable path to avoid the worst of the mud. Follow this track for nearly a mile and, when you reach the crossroads entirely surrounded by woodland, take the track to the right, which, after a very short distance, bears slightly to the right. Continue straight ahead as the track starts to descend the hill.

The downhill that follows is a right little trials section and fair game, especially if it's been raining. At the bottom of this section, join the tarmac drive until you hit the

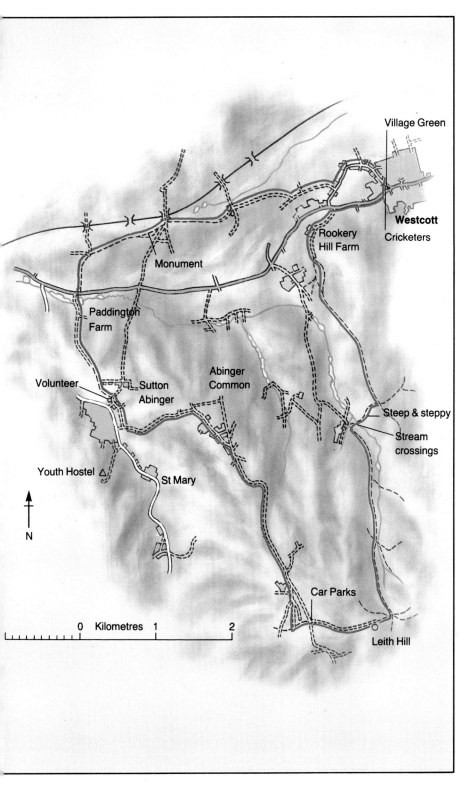

T-junction. Turn left, and enjoy this pootling stuff for the next mile or so, because it's a long gradual climb on a well-used, hard-surfaced track. On reaching the head of this track, you'll find a woodland 'Seven Dials': take the right uphill, and see if you can get all the way up to the top of Leith Hill, where there is a tower and wonderful views (weather permitting), and perhaps the *refreshment booth* will be open!

After your well earned glug of tea and chomp of cake, take the track diametrically opposite your approach and bash on down, taking the left fork till you come to the car parks and the road, though be careful on this last bit because it can be popular with the foot brigade.

Using the Green Cross Code, cross the road and follow the bridleway more or less straight ahead. Where the field ends, turn right on to the well-used track. Continue until the road is close by on your right; this bridleway now runs parallel to the road, past High Ashes Farm, and straight ahead. As the road starts to veer away, you'll pass the entrance to 'Dorlin' and a high hedge on your left. Again dive into woods, when the path turns into one of those classic gulleys so often found in this part of the world, and as usual, it's deep mud along the bottom. However, you can use the left-hand bank, which will demand a little careful balance but is usually fairly dry. After this little exercise, you soon reach road again by Park House Farm and now you follow the road (boo) for a while.

Follow the road, ignoring the first set of junctions, but taking the left road after about half a mile, where there is a well in the middle of the fork. At the next junction, after about ¾ mile, turn left again and continue past a turning on your left, where folks starting form Holmbury St Mary Youth Hostel will be joining the route. Ride on down to Sutton Abinger, where you should turn right in front of the Volunteer (or straight on into it if the fancy takes you), and just beyond the pub turn left up a steep tarmac drive. This drive soon decays into a rough track with grass growing along the ever pop'lar 'central ridge'.

At the end don't go through the gate but turn right alongside the fence and out into the field. Following the right-hand edge of this field, bear left where a footpath crosses and in another fifty yards or so, the path runs between two fences, down towards Paddington Farm. Once reached, turn left into the yard and almost immediately right, following the concrete road between the farm buildings. As you leave these, the road swings to the left, and then to the right around a silted-up mill pond with the old mill on your left and watercress beds beyond the trees.

A little way ahead is the A25, which you have to cross. It's a busy road, so beware. Take the gully opposite, where the locals chuck their rubbish to signal their appreciation of its rustic charm. Continue to the gate. After passing through and securing it, head across the pasture and into the woods opposite. Here the path continues to the right and goes through another gate; this is 'Broomy Downs' and 'Abinger Roughs'. Wonderful woodlands, and so popular that it is a maze of well-trodden paths. Stick to the main one, until it follows the edge of the wood, with fields on your left. You may catch sight of a train or two – they're getting there. Somewhat further on is a group of farm buildings to your left, with a commemorative cross by the path on the right. The inscription is brief and interesting.

Continue on your way, crossing the lane and taking the path at the edge of the woods with a barbed wire fence on the left. After a short distance, this path takes a sharp right and a sharp left to follow the edge of the field, until you reach the farm which has been visible ahead. Follow down between the barns and turn right along the track between two fields and opposite the front of the farmhouse you just passed. There are a few junctions ahead, but simply continue in roughly the same direction and keeping to the main track, which eventually turns into a tarmac lane. Finally, this lane takes a turn to the right and you come down to a T-junction, where you should turn left to follow the lane back to the village green. This has been a posh off-road ride.

Location
Chilterns, Buckinghamshire

Start
Wendover railway station

Distance
overall   17.7 km/11 miles
road   5.6 km/3.5 miles
rough   12.1 km/7.5 miles

Terrain
Wooded chalk escarpment; steep
scarp with ridge and valley-dip slope

Going
Mixture of chalk, clay and flint;
several steep hills; very muddy
throughout winter and spring

Maps
O.S. Landranger sheet 165
O.S. Pathfinder sheet SP 80/90

First catch your train, if that be your mode of transport, at Marylebone or Baker Street in London, or at any of the intermediate stops on the Chiltern Line. Alighting at Wendover (having drooled over the terrain after leaving the urbanity of the metrollops) turn right out of the station and right again at the top of the slope. Continue uphill on this road until it takes a sharp turn to the right, when you'll see a track leading off to the left with the ever pop'lar 'Ridgeway Path' sign pointing along it. When you reach the barrier take the bridleway (leftmost track) and plod on up. This is a long gradual climb, the first few yards being a bit tricky, but it soon becomes easier. It's worth stopping for a breather when you see the trees begin to thin, because there is a good view over the 'Vale of Aylesbury'.

Having reached the top, when the track starts to level off a bit, and veers slightly to the left, you'll see a stile in the fence ahead and here you should turn right, down a fairly steep gully. Watch out for walkers crossing (about halfway down) and take care – there's a busy road at the bottom where you must make a sharp left turn, through the gate, and follow the track alongside the golf course to regain some of the elevation so recently lost. Deviate neither to the left nor right until you reach road again; turn left and left again a few yards on at the junction. Just up here, turn first right on to the bridleway. Taking the lower of the two paths, pedal on, even when it becomes a little indistinct (after a mile or so), until it joins another track at right angles, were you should turn right until, after a short distance, you reach a blind lane. Turn left and continue in the direction of the lane after it ends, and across Little Hampden Common.

On emerging from the common you'll find lunch, in the shape of the Rising Sun, a little ahead on your right.

When you're quite ready to crank yourself into action again, take the bridleway going down at an angle into the woods opposite the pub. This is generally quite waterlogged, but firm underwheel. It takes a few slight turns as it goes downhill, but beware – there's a megaboghole at the bottom which you will have to cross one way or another – to the uphill track on the other side. At the top, turn right along the ridge; after rain this is a mudpluggers paradise, except for this last section, where it runs alongside a meadow, which will be when my ears start to burn.

This track soon becomes a lane, and the lane comes out on to a green: you must take the track which continues the same line – the entrance to which is not overly evident. Again, continue along the ridge, that is to say: if you're going downhill, you're lost. This track joins a lane for a short way, and after this look out for a pine wood ahead. On the other side of the wood, the track has a dogleg, with your track heading down into the valley to the left (or straight on, depending on your point of view). This downhill is best in winter because of rampant nettles in the summer; it's flinty, with a twist towards the bottom.

Under the railway bridge and along to the end; we now embark upon the really dangerous section... the dreased A413 and the infernal combusiton engine. Take your life in your hands for just on *Kilometto*, turning right into Bowood Lane and sanity again.

When you come to the Antique Shop turn right. This is a fairly long uphill, but, being tarmac, is not too uncivilized besides which it is little used and even less maintained, thus not too unlike proper off-road. On gaining the top of this ridge, and the junction, turn left and follow this ridgetop lane along to Kingsash, were you turn left again, and, by a white house on your right, turn right inot a bridleway directed to Concord. Follow this until the farm track veers off to the right and

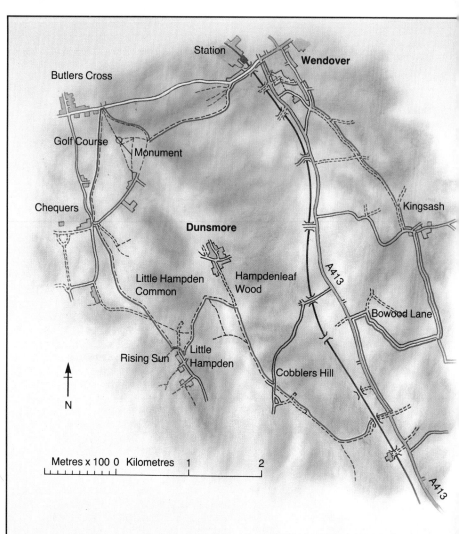

the mudbath to the left (there's a slightly easier path running parallel on the left, beyond the bank). This is a sunken path, very popular with the Jaunters, and known by us as 'Concord Gorge'. It winds its way down the scarp and opens into Hogtrough Lane – a farm access lane that has happily been surfaced with half-bricks.

At the end you are back in Wendover and the best return route to the station is down Dark Lane. Turn right out of Hogtrough Lane and continue uphill, the junction on your right, and on proceeding downhill, look out for the Dark Lane entrance on your left – easily missed at velocity – and follow it to the main road, where you should turn right. When you reach the mini-roundabout turn sharp left for a cup of tea etcetera, or left proper for the station, which is up ahead a few hundred yards and down the slope to your right.

Location
Peak District, Derbyshire

Start
Hayfield

Distance
overall   16 km/10 miles
road   3.2 km/2 miles
rough   12.8 km/8 miles

Terrain
Open hills, rough pasture

Going
Tracks and bridleways; muddy in places; mostly thin soil on rock

Maps
O.S. Landranger sheet 110
O.S. Pathfinder sheet SK 08/18

After learning about cross-country cycling on a really enjoyable YHA course, I decided, as a result, to buy a mountain bike. So last Christmas I sprung the cash and took home a nice white Muddy Fox Courier, fitting only mudguards and waterbottle.

During the Christmas vac from university I spent a lot of time looking for suitable rides in the area around my house, up with this one, based around Hayfield.

It's a totally legal ride using bridleways, and as there is an extensive network of them in this area, there is plenty of scope for longer or shorter rides. However, this one took me between three and four hours.

The ride starts at Brookhouse Farm, on the left as you travel north on the A624, about 1½ miles out of Hayfield.

The lane we want turns off the main road where there is a slight dip, the main road going off to the right, and our lane dropping quite sharply past Brookhouse Farm, then climbing up, over a cattle-grid, towards Matleymoor Farm. Our lane becomes a track at the point where it turns a sharp left and starts a short, gradual descent to a bridleway, where you should again turn left, especially if the sign says that it goes to Birch Vale.

This bridleway goes through the gate in the corner of the field and there is a short, sharp uphill ahead. Further on, take the lower, more level track by the wall; the path now skirts round Lantern Pike, and continues downhill, under some trees, past a house on the right – and watch out, there's a crossroads with a minor country lane. Cross over and continue ahead and down until you reach the main road at the bottom, in Birch Vale.

Turn left, and, having crossed the River Sett – about fifty yards – turn immediate right. This track soon crosses the 'Sett Valley Cycle Trail', based on the route of a disused railway track – worth using if you are a very beginner cross-country cyclist – but, for today, we cross over and head up the small path between the trees opposite. Yes, this is still a bridleway, even though it goes through a park. At the top of the park there is a ramp which exists on to the A6015. Turn left here and right after about 100 yards, by some railings. You should soon pass some houses to your right and quarries to your left. The track turns fairly sharply left, and here the long gradual climb begins. Also the surface of the way degrades somewhat and becomes quite bumpy. Stick with it… there's worse to come.

After about one and a half miles of gradual climb you'll reach a crossroads, with a blind lane to the right, bridleways ahead and to the left. Take the left-hand bridleway, through the gates, and brace yourself for a longish, steep and tricky climb.

Gaining the top of the hill, turn left by the post and ride alongside the wall. The path is later flanked by a wall on both sides. This is about the halfway mark, so if the weather's fine, atop this hill is as good a place as any for lunch.

Continue through the gates and, as the path bears to the right, look out for a signpost and take the track to your left. Now we have about a mile and a half of pure downhill. After a short distance there is a path joining from the left, and at this point you should be able to see a transmitter mast some way straight ahead. Fork right here, and fork right again at the next junction. This is a steep, tricky downhill section following the line of Foxholes Clough.

You will have to pass through two gates before going through Phoside Farmyard. Keep right, go through the gate, and turn left down the track until you reach the main road (A624). Go straight across and up the steep road opposite. Turn left at the top. This minor road runs parallel to the main road and brings you into Hayfield without fumes. After you've crossed the river, turn right by the Post Office on your left, with a pub on your right.

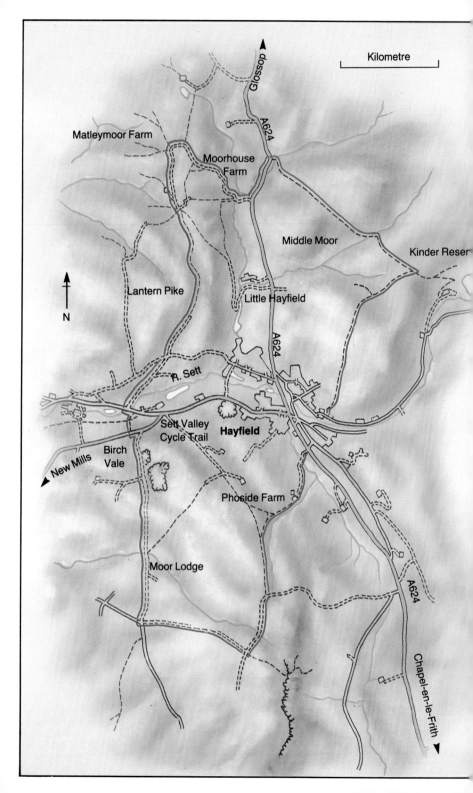

Continue up the hill until you see a signpost to your left for 'Snake Inn via William Clough'. Turn up here and through the gate as the track bends to the right.

Head on along this track, through the numerous gates, until you can see two small white shooting cabins ahead and a National Trust sign. Go through yet another gate and continue towards the two buildings, turning left over a footbridge before you reach them. Follow this path, along which is a challenging ford, and in due course you'll see the road ahead. Turn left on to the main road and in a very short while you'll see the lane at which this ride started.

John Summerscales

Location
Llansantffraed Cwdenddwr

Start
Devil's Bridge or Rhayader

Distance
overall   41.5 km/25.8 miles
road   8.5 km/5.3 miles
rough   33 km/20.5 miles

Terrain
High moor with reservoirs

Going
Mountain tracks with bog in places

Maps
O.S. Landranger sheet 147
O.S. Pathfinder sheets SN 87/97 and SN 86/96

The closest town is Rhayader, from where you should take the B4518, past Elan Village and the Dam until, with the reservoir on your left, the road follows the headland round to the right and there is a bridge on your left across the reservoir. At this point you join the route.

Alternatively, if you want to travel to the area by train, you will need to go via Shrewsbury and Aberystwyth to Devil's Bridge (BR timetables 75 & 73), from where you take the B4343 as far as Ffair Rhos, when you should take the lane going due east up on to the moors.

If travelling by car to this starting-point, then park somewhere along here; continue ahead and the lane will become 'unsuitable for motor vehicles', just what we've been waiting for...

This track gradually drops down to run alongside the Claerwen Reservoir, when it becomes somewhat more distinct.

On reaching the Dam, take the road until it becomes walled or fenced and where, according to the map, there is, of all things, an AA phone box. At this point there is a RUPP veering off to your left. Take this up over the pass. Be sure to follow it round the hill to your right, towards the forest. It traverses the forest edge and enters it after about half a mile, going downhill to the bridge over the Garreg Ddu Reservoir.

This is the alternative starting point.

Crossing the bridge, turn left and follow the road alongside the reservoir for about 1½ miles; take the track that runs parallel to, and slightly above, the road. This track takes you past one dam and follows the north side of Pen-y-garreg Reservoir. When you come to the next dam, with the public conveniences, cross it and turn right, following the road in a westerly, then northerly, direction past Hirnant.

At spot height 347m look out for the 'Ancient Road' RUPP doubling back to your right. This high moor route achieves a height of 542m, or 1778 ft in English, and is boggy and indistinct at times. For all that it is fabulous XC-cycling terrain and affords spectacular views.

This section of the route is about 6½ miles long, and you will eventually join the track that runs down into the Claerwen valley. If you came up this way then turn right for your return, or turn left for a return to Rhayader ... or for a second circuit!

Sowell Kinley

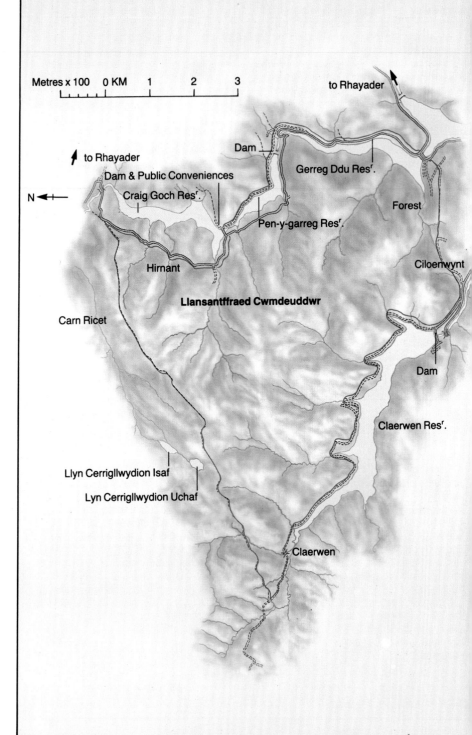

Location
Quantock Hills, Somerset

Start
Holford Village

Distance
overall 27 km/16.8 miles
road —
rough 27 km/16.8 miles

Terrain
Wooded combes, rising to hill tops
with bracken and heather

Going
Rough stony paths; stream cros-
sings; no bogs

Maps
O.S. Landranger sheet 181
O.S. Pathfinder sheets ST 04/14 and
ST 03/13

The Quantocks are riddled with bridleways, so this route is quite legit.

Now then, you really need a car or stamina for this one, because you'll have to do an extra 27.3km (17 miles) if you take the train to Taunton and ride up from there. It's about the same from Bridgewater station, but, it being a smaller station, fewer trains stop there… You *could* make a weekend of it though, couldn't you?

Anyway, park your bike transporter in the large lay-by just above Holford village… Approaching along the A39 from Bridgewater to Minehead, it's to your left on a wide, sweeping right-hand bend, about half a mile before Holford.

There's a small tarmac lane off the lay-by which leads to Holford Combe. Take this for about ten yards and turn left on to a bridleway signed 'To Crowcombe'.

Ride up this hill until it meets some deciduous woods on your right. Look out for a narrow path into these woods. Take it until you emerge, after a gentle descent, on to a more clearly defined track into Holford Combe.

Follow the course of the stream along Holford Combe, which involves crossing the stream several times (yippee), until you reach the parting of the combes; into Lady's Combe and Frog Combe. Now, don't take either of these, but head, more or less straight on, slightly to your right, up a very loose steep stony track.

After getting up there *somehow*, this track levels out and becomes grassy.

Continue ahead, going straight over the crossing with another track, and skirt Wilmot's Pool to your left before a short descent towards a tarmac lane. Avoid the road (*at all costs*) by forking right to Crowcombe Park Gate, and left to Crowcombe Combe Gate. Cross the lane and follow the track along the ridge to Triscombe Stone, where there is a car park.

Pass Triscombe Stone and the track now borders a coniferous plantation. When it begins to rise and becomes stony, fork right, pass a junction, and fork right again at the next. This will bring you to 'Pit (disused)'. Here you can prove the map wrong by using said pit for all kinds of unmentionable antics, but not lunch … yet.

All good things must come to an end; so mount your steed and head off up the path which runs alongside the pit. This takes you to the highest point in the Quantocks; 'Wills Neck'. And the view to be had from here makes it the spot for lunch.

Suitably refreshed, continue ahead until the path begins its descent in earnest, when a right turn will bring you back down to Triscombe Stone. Look out for your tyre tracks and retrace your previous route as far as Crowcombe Park Gate, then continue on this broad track along the ridge, keeping to the newly erected fence, up over Hurley Beacon, past Halsway Soggs, past Halsway Post and on to Bicknoller Post, being sure to veer right at Lowsey Thorn.

By continuing in this direction you'll cross 'The Great Road', which is, in fact, a trackway, and, cresting Beacon Hill, look for a grassy track to your right. Take this and, after a short distance, descend to the left of a small coniferous plantation.

This delightful descent is considered one of the best in the Quantocks. It is quite steep and stony until you ford the stream and enter Smith's Combe, which you should follow right to the bottom, savouring every moment, diving in and out of the stream as you go.

When Smith's Combe begins to open out into the valley, and crosses the stream for the last time, turn right and climb round the ridge. Keeping pasture to your left and rough to your right, down into, and up out of, Dens Combe, fork right soon after. Head due south

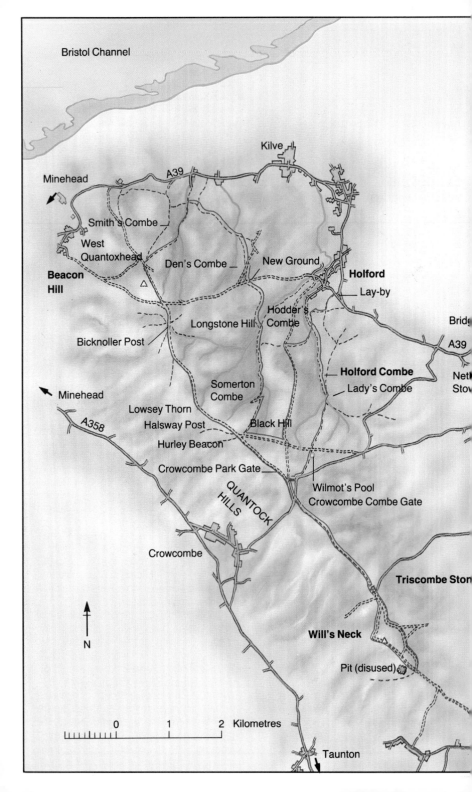

until you reach New Ground; go straight across, bearing left and taking the track that skirts Longstone Hill, on down into Hodder's Combe and through the river.

At this point you can take a short-cut home by turning left and lopping some 5 km, or about three miles, off this route.

But we know you'll be wanting more.

So, turn right and go up to the combe until you reach the next ford. Here, take the left fork up an ill-defined path along Somerton Combe. Up the headland where Stert Combe joins Somerton Combe, ascend, first climbing at an angle veering to the right, then making a zig-zag, left along the contour and right up along the ridge.

At the top you'll come to a T-junction at which you should turn left, following this track, past two paths to the left, until you reach a cross-tracks, with the left arm running along the spine of Black Hill. Take this, passing Higher Hare Knap to your left. Continue downhill until the grassy track levels out slightly and you come to the next cross-tracks. Turn right.

This descent will bring you down with a splash into Holford Combe again. But a little cautionary note here ... there is a BOG, a small one perhaps, but a real live genuine lesser-spotted Bog. (For the cheats I will tell you that it can be avoided by skirting round to the left.)

At this point you have four options: (1) turn right for a second lap; (2) turn left for Holford Village and welcome refreshment; (3) retrace your tyre tracks up the other side of the combe to return to the car park; and (4) go to a beach party.

Tim Flooks

▶PREVENTION◀

There is an inviolable rule for all outdoor sports which carry an element of risk – **you don't behave in a manner which increases the risk to yourself, to members of your party, or to others who may follow.**

Mountain biking is risky to start with.

Balancing a bike on uneven terrain requires skill and concentration in good weather, and more of the same when the conditions deteriorate. One of the first elements of safe behaviour is anticipation of what weather conditions are possible, and planning to cope with them.

This is particularly true of exposed and isolated rides. High moorland can be a soft delight in warm, clear conditions, but is notorious for sudden changes of weather which can affect temperature, visibility and the effort needed to propel the bike along. Inexperienced riders should never venture far from a metalled road if such a weather change is likely, and in any event, they should always be accompanied by more seasoned riders until they have acquired sufficient personal survival skills and local knowledge.

This advice is ignored every year by some who venture forth on moorland, with exposure, injury, loss of life, and extreme risk to rescue teams among the consequences of their irresponsibility. It isn't possible to best-guess the weather on every occasion, so when you're planning a long ride in isolated, rough country, anticipate the worst, and take precautions.

Always let someone responsible know where you are going and when you are expected back.

Check all your equipment carefully before starting out. Don't set out if anything is not functioning correctly – on you or the bike.

Take basic navigational equipment – map, compass and a light.

As emergency repair equipment, take tools and a puncture outfit – and know how to use both!

Take a basic first-aid kit, with adequate bandage, plaster and antiseptic to staunch, clean and bind a serious flesh wound. Pain killers, insect bite and sun screen preparations are also essential.

Always take emergency rations, such as chocolate or Kendal Mint Cake; you need calories in a survival situation, so hang the teeth and the diet!

Have large, full drinks containers, with water in at least one. You may need it for more than drinking.

Fit lights and have back-up batteries.

If there is the remotest chance of being stranded overnight, have a small tent for preference, but at least a bivouac bag and a sleeping bag. If you possess neither, then a large garden refuse bag or two will keep you dry and warm overnight (but don't put polythene over your head!).

Take a change of clothing.

Take writing material and strong, weatherproof adhesive tape. Then if you have to abandon the bike and try to walk out, you can attach a message to the bike, preferably in a plastic bag, telling when you left and in what direction.

Never go without a watch and fire-lighting equipment.

This may sound like a lot of extra weight, and it will certainly fill a pannier or a rucksack, but set against a life, it ain't heavy!

Never be reluctant to change plans if weather looks adverse, or if a rider begins to suffer. A pleasant day's riding rapidly becomes a nightmare if bad visibility and cold conspire to strand a party in hostile terrain. If one of you is injured or ill, or just plain exhausted, the problem can become life-threatening very quickly.

Democracy is no help in survival situations. To have a team leader with experience of both the terrain and the sport is essential if you're going to reach sensible decisions in an emergency. Emergencies are not fitting subjects for debate – precious time can be wasted in dissension. Wise action is what's needed; analysis can wait.

Research, like reconnaissance, is never a waste of time before you ride a difficult or dangerous route. Know what territory is to be encountered, its degree of severity and whether there are shorter 'escape routes' in case of bad weather or injury.

Try to develop basic navigational skills, so you can plot rough position during rides. This might be essential in deciding whether to return, press on, or stay put and wait for help in an emergency. There is no golden rule, but common sense dictates that, in bad weather, the shortest route out is usually the one to choose. However, if there is dangerous ground behind and in front and visibility is bad, stay put and wait for help.

▶ Coping with an emergency ◀

If you're forced to bivouac, choice of ground is important. Obviously, you need shelter from prevailing winds. Wind-chill is the precursor of exposure (hypothermia), which is one of the biggest dangers to people stranded in the open. Seek rocks or low walls, but avoid lying in hollows which might fill with water in a rainstorm.

There is a drill which should be known and practised by all who venture into the wilder places. Here is a broad outline.

EVALUATE the situation, decide on the best course of action to remove the immediate danger, and carry the action out.

RELAX into the new circumstances and take stock of surroundings and resources (food and drink, shelter, means of creating warmth or cold, necessary tasks to sustain survival). This has the dual purpose of overcoming any tendency to panic, and ensuring that the group leader can see how each individual adjusts to the new situation.

PLAN for the group's immediate survival and longer-term removal from danger. This may be complicated by the fact that a member of the party is injured, and so needs more urgent action than the rest of the party. This is most acute when the party consists of just two people, and the agonizing choice between going for help or staying to help the injured person has to be made. A calm and measured decision is absolutely vital in such a case, so do not rush it. Build a fire or a shelter, or go for some water in order to ease the tension of the first moments, then start confronting the facts rationally.

Mountain biking is a sport for independent, adventurous cyclists. Such people tend to be loners, but over the years a number of national organizations for cyclists who like to stray from the beaten track have developed. The most relevant of these to the off-road cyclist are the Mountain Bike Club, the British Cyclo-Cross Association, the Cross-Country Cycling Club, the Cyclists' Touring Club, and the Rough Stuff Fellowship.

▶Mountain Bike Club◀

The Mountain Bike Club is run by mountain bikers for mountain bikers, and involves itself at every level, from answering simple queries to promoting a national championship. However, it is primarily an organization for exchanging information. It is a network through which off-road cyclists, ATB riders and mountain bikers can share knowledge.

The club can give access to members who have been mountain biking in Borneo, Iceland, Ascension Island, Africa, America, Australasia and throughout Europe. The informal network is available to all members, and invaluable to those planning an expedition.

The Mountain Bike Club is based in Telford in Shropshire and describes the advantages of membership as follows.

- Third-party insurance up to £500,000.
- Access to the Mountain Bike Club information network. The MBC has a twenty-four hour Hotline and an active correspondence section which deals with queries of all kinds.
- An extensive library of bicycle test reports written by mountain bikers.
- The newsletter, *Mountain Biking*, delivered to every member, at least quarterly.
- The MBC runs training weekends in historic Ironbridge Gorge, Shropshire. They cover most off-road bicycle-handling skills. The courses are only open to members, and proficiency certificates are awarded.
- Discount scheme. Certain shops throughout the UK offer discounts on components and even on complete bikes to MBC members. Holiday centres for off-road riders also offer discount on bike hire, accommodation and guided tours of some beautiful areas. One centre will even give MBC members free use of its workshop if they are in the vicinity. The discount scheme is growing and new offers are added regularly.
- Free advertising. All advertising in the club newsletter originates from the members, who use the pages free. There is a lively trade in second-hand bikes, components, and equipment.
- Expedition contacts. Leaders of mountain bike expeditions to all parts of the world use the newsletter to recruit.
- Local and national contacts. Members wishing to find other riders and share routes can receive the names and addresses of fellow off-road riders, in their neighbourhood or elsewhere in the country.
- International contacts. The MBC has members all over the world who are keen to show riders the best parts of their countries and to give advice about off-road riding.
- Local club network. As an umbrella organization, the Mountain Bike Club is attracting more and more local mountain bike clubs as they spring up. If there is a local group of enthusiasts, the MBC encourages the formation of regional clubs to serve the area.
- National calendar. The Mountain Bike Club publishes a national calendar of off-road meetings and events, updated constantly. As more and more events spring up round the country, the calendar keeps riders informed of new races, meetings and rides. The club co-ordinates events throughout Britain, so that clashes are averted and all mountain bikers can enjoy the maximum number of rallies and meetings.

- Fun rides. During the year the MBC organizes fun rides for riders of all standards, in all parts of the country. MBC fun rides are relaxed and friendly events, ideal for novices because the pace is easy. Mountain bike orienteering is growing in popularity among the non-competitive fun riders.
- Races. The Mountain Bike Club endorses races throughout the UK. Often these are organized by local members with permission from a local landowner. The MBC helps to publicize these events and advises on circuit design, safety measures and entry levels.
- National championships. The MBC has organized the UK national championships since 1984. Until 1987 they were always one-off, low-key affairs, with a friendly atmosphere and a small group of regular riders. Things changed in 1988, when mountain biking grew enormously in popularity. The Mountain Bike Club attracted a major sponsor, Shimano, the largest bicycle components manufacturer in the world. The championships were held in six locations across the UK, and established the first large-scale mountain bike series in the country. Events attracted more than 200 entries, and special categories for juniors, seniors and men and women were established. Trade-sponsored teams from Fisher, Specialized, Peugeot, Marin/Carlsberg, Muddy Fox, Schmoo's, Overbury's, Beta Bikes, Barretto's, *Bicycle Action*, Two Wheels Good and Avon Valley Cyclery took part, along with hundreds of private racers, MBC members and others.
- Access campaigns. Mountain biking is a new sport and is seen as a threat by many other country users. The Mountain Bike Club is a responsible body which tries to make mountain bikers aware of their responsibilities in the countryside. The publication of the *Off-road Code* in 1984 has been credited with much success in making sure mountain bikers do not get banned from country areas. The club has also established close links with the Countryside Commission, and has negotiated rights of access to private land for mountain bikers in several parts of the countryside.
- Affiliation to the Byways and Bridleways Trust. Membership includes automatic affiliation to BBT, an organization which protects the rights of all country visitors.
- Special purchases. Having good links with the cycle industry means the club can get hold of some discontinued stock. Anything which it buys is passed on to members at cost price plus postage. This means that useful components and extras which are no longer carried by retailers can sometimes be obtained through the MBC.
- Club equipment. The MBC supports its activities through the sale of items branded with the club's logo, from clothing to bike accessories. Unusual equipment, such as adjustable goggles, is also available to MBC members only.
- Holidays. The club runs holidays for members who wish to explore different counties or countries.
- Workshop facilities. A fully equipped workshop, with experienced mechanics on hand, is open to all club members.

Mountain Bike Club
3 The Shrubbery
Albert Street
St Georges
Telford
Shropshire TF2 9AS

▶ British Cyclo-cross Association ◀

Primarily a winter sport, cyclo-cross is a form of cross-country cycle racing, in which the competitor rides where possible, and runs with the bike where the going makes it impossible to ride. The machines used are road-racing bikes, and the courses are usually one or two miles long, lapped several times. They are often situated in parks.

Cyclo-cross is an international sport with an unusual status. Because the international cycle sport regulatory bodies designate it a 'pastime', amateur and professional riders can compete together in cyclo-cross. Mountain bikers have taken part in cyclo-cross events, and some cyclo-cross riders also compete in (and win!) mountain bike races. Interestingly, the ATB is not as fast over the typical cyclo-cross route as the pure racing mount. This is because the mountain bike is designed to go almost anywhere, whereas the main feature of cyclo-cross routes is mud! However, the two sports are developing a strong mutual respect and closer links are bound to result.

British Cyclo-cross Association
Geoff Mayne
208 Ecclesall Road
Sheffield S11 8JD

Cross-country Cycling Club

In many ways an alternative Mountain Bike Club, this organization has common beginnings with the MBC, since the organizers were, along with the organizers of the MBC, founders of the National Off-road Bicycle Association in the early 1980s. NORBA is the governing body of the sport in the US, but its British equivalent did not thrive, and now the Cross-country Cycling Club concerns itself with the interests of all 'adventurous cyclists'.

Publishing a regular and popular magazine, *Making Tracks*, which is an excellent source of information about ATB routes, technical matters and off-road cycling affairs, the organization is keen to help mountain biking establish a strong appeal across all sections of the community, and not just those who wish to race or pose. Currently the club is putting most of its efforts into ensuring that people who wish to ride off-road are able to get access, find others of like mind, and ride regularly. They have been very successful in this, and fifteen monthly rides are organized

around the country, with these basic features:

- each ride takes place on the same Sunday, monthly
- meeting time is 10.30 a.m. for an 11 a.m. start
- where possible, start locations are near railway stations and food shops or a café
- rides are between 10 and 20 miles, over moderate terrain, and the needs of less experienced riders in any group are favoured. The routes range between 3 and 4 miles from the start-point, to enable riders to cut back early if necessary, and the ride usually finishes by 4 p.m. In the summer, further rides may be organized into the evening.

Such initiatives as this one are crucial if mountain biking is to become more than a fringe sport. Indeed, the existence of such an organization as the Cross-country Cycling Club would be desirable even if there were a fully national, established and thriving competitive side to mountain biking, for it draws new blood into the sport, whilst at the same time keeping a place for the older rider, the less competitive and those for whom the social aspect is paramount. On the other hand, it would be wrong to assume that sport is ignored by the Cross-country Cycling Club, since it is the body which develops and organizes the trials scene in mountain biking, and this type of competition attracts a good following.

Cross-country Cycling Club
5 Old Station Cottages
Ford
Arundel
West Sussex BN18 0BJ

Cyclists' Touring Club

The largest on-road cycle organization in the UK, with 40,000 members, but with a marginal interest in mountain biking. However, the CTC is a powerful lobby for cycling as whole, and

Rough Stuff Fellowship

This group of hardy cycle tourists have quietly been riding conventional bicycles on off-road or extremely out-of-the-way routes for years. Specializing in long-distance touring, and drawing on a thirty-year tradition, the Fellowship has a network of local groups, a regular magazine and much knowledge of use to those who wish to venture further a field than the local moor or bog.

membership is a good idea for any rider who wants to participate in foreign touring.

Cyclists' Touring Club
69 Meadrow
Godalming
Surrey

Rough Stuff Fellowship
9 Liverpool Avenue
Southport PR8 3NE

To look at the majority of advertising for mountain bikes, or read the editorial in most magazines covering the subject, you could get the impression that this is a fringe sport for the very young, very fit or very weird.

Nothing could be further from the truth. In fact, the enhanced safety and stability, low maintenance, durability and go-anywhere capability of the mountain bike actually make it a better choice of machine for the casual pleasure user than other types of mock-racer or touring bike.

It is a pity that the marketing gurus of the UK cycle trade have (with some notable exceptions) chosen to promote the machines, in the late 1980s, to the extremely fashion-conscious segment of the buying public. They are denying themselves a wider public and greater sales, and may find that the people to whom they have directed such expensive hype will desert them for some other fad in a year or so, leaving a lot of bikes in dealers' showrooms. There is a place for the competition-minded, and for extreme, race-bred machinery. It is from such machines that the product development which improves the breed for everyday use springs. But it is not all the market, and it is fortunate that the ranges of Raleigh, Dawes, Peugeot, Giant and Muddy Fox continue to offer some machines of gentler geometry and more forgiving handling, at an affordable price. Such products are vital to the growth of the *pastime* – rather than the *sport* – of mountain biking, and both aspects are important if mountain biking is to have a healthy future.

So what does the mountain bike have to offer to those users who are not thinking of sport – ranging from pre-driving-age youngsters commuting to school or job to older riders wanting to stay fit and committed cycle tourists who want to travel far and wide? The answer is simple. Plenty. Correctly equipped, the ATB will handle every cycling task except out-and-out road racing with perfect efficiency, and a great deal of comfort.

The bikes are particularly adaptable to long-distance touring, and can live a rather more knockabout existence than some of the beautiful, but rather frail, thoroughbred tourers sold today. Indeed, these derivatives of the road-racing machine are better suited to high-speed race training than the rigours of long-distance touring, particularly when you take into account the kind of handling meted out to them in transit on ferries and in aeroplanes. ATB tyres, especially the versatile narrower knobblies with the smooth centre strip, are also ideally suited to touring, and can be obtained in versions with tough composite inserts to make them practically puncture-proof in most uses.

At the heart of the matter is the incomparably wide gearing of the mountain bike, which ensures that, although not the fastest of bikes, it will always get there, whatever the gradient. Not everyone will be plotting routes across the Kalahari, through the Andes, or into equatorial jungles – although all these things have been done on mountain bikes. Some young families will be looking for pleasure transport for mum, dad and a couple of kids; mountain bikes are available with the sort of specification that is as well-thought-out for the children's machines as for the adults'. The 'Mixte' frame, which has a slightly sloping twin-top-tube arrangement, makes a very viable women's machine, but the generally smaller frame sizes of mountain bikes ensure that most women and girls will feel quite at home on the small men's version.

▶ PURSUIT CENTRES, BIKE HIRE ◀ AND BIKING HOLIDAYS

As the leisure industry develops, so more and more centres start to cater for specialized pursuits. Mountain biking has already begun to be accepted as a growth sport, with a number of facilities around the country catering both for confirmed enthusiasts and for those wishing to try it for the first time.

New centres are springing up all the time; the best way to select a place to suit you is to buy a copy of *Bicycle Action* and survey the ads, or join the Mountain Bike Club or Cross-country Cycling Club (or both, they are very inexpensive), and take advantage of their information exchange.

A variety of different packages are available. They can offer planned routes or single-day centres, such as Rutland Water, where a cycle track has been established round the giant 3,000-acre reservoir. Rutland is already a well-developed centre for yachting, sailboarding, game fishing and birdwatching, and the enterprising management has seen the potential for cycling round the perimeter of Europe's largest artificial lake. Bikes can be hired from two shops around the reservoir, and although Rutland is not strictly a mountain bike centre, ATBs *are* available, and they make a very suitable form of transport for the scenic route. Rutland is a perfect day's outing in its own right, or it could be a familiarization exercise for those contemplating a longer cycling

One of Rutland Water's bike hire shops – there is also an ATB track

tour off-road. Facilities abound for picnics, buying food and enjoying the lovely East-Midlands location to the full. Rides around Rutland range from 2 to 25 miles, and fifteen-speed mountain bikes are available for hire for as little as £4.50 for three hours, or £8.50 all day. The selection of bicycle types for hire embraces every conventional category, including BMX, tandems and adult tricycle. Full information for planning a really enjoyable day out is available from D.J. & A.D. Archer, Rutland Water Cycling, Whitwell Car Park, Oakham, Rutland (078086 705).

Near London, Action Packs offer a two-day tour in the Surrey Hills, including bike hire, accommodation for one night and a guide, for around £40 (0306 886944). Guided one-day tours in the south Chilterns can be had from Ancient Treks, £40 inclusive of bike hire, while a four-day unaccompanied ride on the Wessex Ridgeway costs £130, inclusive of bike hire and accommodation.

On Dartmoor, Adventure Cycles (0626 862706) offer a weekend riding on mixed terrain for £50, (bike hire extra). In Wales, Clive Powell Mountain Bikes, based in Rhayader, Powys (0597 810585), offer everything from a half-day hire to a residential week (Saturday to Saturday), with prices ranging from £8 to £145. This includes accommodation and can incorporate training courses in riding, bike maintenance and racing.

Mountain Bike Dales Tours (0748 811885) offer bike hire and tours ranging from an evening to a weekend, with prices from £4.50 to £75. In Scotland, bikes can be hired from Hill Craft (09752 207) for use in both the Grampians and Cairngorms, and from Perthshire Mountain Bikes, located on the shores of Loch Tay (08873 291).

Special adventure holidays which include mountain biking are available in Cornwall through Outdoor Adventure, Widemouth Bay (028885 312); other sports available on the same holiday – all under expert instruction – are windsurfing, canoeing and rock climbing.

This is only a selection of the mountain biking routes and facilities open to the novice and inexperienced rider. Of course, more opportunities are becoming available all the time, and the best idea is to keep an eye on the mountain bike press and send off for literature as new centres and courses are advertised. It is not only in Britain that such facilities exist. Mountain biking is very popular in France and good opportunities exist in some of the less well-known areas of Spain, and the US – where it all began – has tremendous facilities. The conditioning factor is your budget. Information isn't difficult to come by, if you use the networks operated both by the Mountain Bike Club and the Cross-country Cycling Club.

▶*PROJECTS*◀

It is surprising how quickly a local route can become familiar, which means you begin to need longer forays, with different scenery, to get the essential variety to sustain your interest. There are two ways of dealing with this: you can go further afield, or you can devise projects which will add interest to the ride.

Projects can range fairly widely. To many, the priority will always be to gain greater fitness and expertise, either for competition or just for personal satisfaction. If this is the case for you, the most important thing to establish is the basis for measurement, so that you can monitor your improvement over a given course or time.

▶*Fitness*◀

A good way to assess your fitness is to select, after research and trial, a course which has a variety of terrain, and whose length you know. To ensure that your riding skill as well as stamina will be improved, it is as well to build in obstacles of varying severity. Streams, logs and steep descents are all useful in this context, but remember that their nature will change dramatically with

weather, and be prepared to make allowances for differing performance according to circumstances. (Indeed, in the interests of personal safety, be prepared to cancel a section out altogether if the weather has made it too dangerous.)

The point of all this is to improve not only the time it takes you to complete the course, but also the levels of expertise with which you negotiate obstacles and the general state of your fitness. There are objective measurements you can take – time of ride, severity of work done, time through difficult sections – as well as subjective ones: does it hurt more or less than the last time? Are anticipation and judgement of difficulty improving? How about reflexes?

If you're in company, these factors can be measured and discussed among the group, and you can help each other to improve. However, the lone rider can also keep tabs on factors as complex as time elapsed, lap or section time, pedal cadence and even personal pulse rate, with one of the several makes of 'on-board computer' now available. For the rider in serious training, the ability to monitor performance that closely is almost essential, but even for the fun rider it can give an added sense of purpose to a regular ride.

▶Photography◀

For some, the mountain bike will be a means to an end, rather than the end itself. Photographers who want to get further off the beaten track than the law or terrain will permit a four-wheel-drive vehicle to go, or even those amateurs who wish to combine hobbies, will find the ATB a real asset. Special camera cases are available to protect the camera and fix it firmly on the rider, to prevent damage and the discomfort of it swinging around. It is amazing how much you can carry in panniers, and the determined wildlife photographer on an ATB can approach the subject far more closely, and with far less of an assault upon the environment, than using almost any mode of transport other than the horse.

As far as photographic subject goes, some find ample subject matter covering the sport itself, and there is a good market among the magazines and books like this one for attractive mountain biking shots of all kinds. Other suitable photographic subjects: birdwatching, landscape, geological and botanical work, historic photography, of both natural and archaeological subjects, and coverage of other outdoor pursuits, such as climbing, orienteering, canoeing, and all the other things that people choose to do in remote places.

With regard to equipment, there are no particular strictures. Obviously, robust but fairly lightweight equipment is ideal, but the constraints of your pocket are the usual limit. Most of the big-name modern 35 mm compact cameras are very good and strong instruments, particularly those designed with outdoor, all-weather use in mind. Modern single-lens reflex 35 mm cameras with largely electronic shutter and exposure control are good, since they have less intricate, moving mechanisms to become dislodged by the rigours of mountain biking – but you should treat any camera as a breakable item, and if you don't possess one of the purpose-made cases for rough stuff use, wrap the camera well and stow it in the middle of a well-packed pannier.

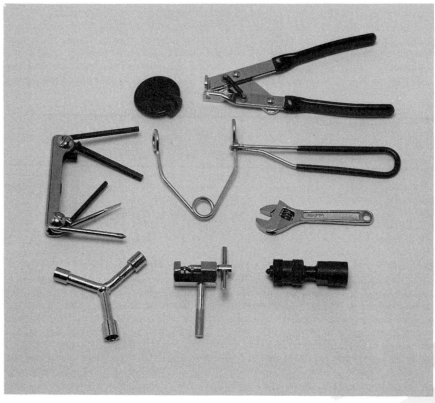

Tools

If you're going to enjoy mountain biking, a certain degree of risk and isolation is almost inevitable. But if you're going to take risks, you have to do some planning. We've already looked at the subject of safety, which should never be overlooked. Any project must have the safety factor planned in, regardless of whether it's a simple matter of not carrying tools in a pocket where they could injure you in a fall, or the more complicated question of mapping out a route to allow for 'fall-backs' in case of bad weather or misadventure.

The planning task obviously increases in complexity as the project in hand becomes more ambitious. Don't be deluded, though, into discarding planning just because you are about to embark on an afternoon jaunt in familiar territory. This is often where the worst accidents occur, as familiarity breeds a contempt which translates into carelessness. Devise a personal checklist, to include taking essential equipment, telling someone where you are going and – that all-important precaution – packing emergency rations and clothing.

▶ Biking abroad ◀

When you are travelling greater distances, over a period of days or weeks, it's obviously impractical to take all the supplies you will need. You need arrangements to provision and supply en route. Your arrangements may be simply taking enough money to purchase food, shelter and necessary equipment on the journey, or you might organize supply dumps ahead, if you're travelling in more primitive surroundings.

Research is the key, especially if you're planning to cross the Sahara or penetrate less-developed areas of the world. You may find yourself dependent on the goodwill of embassy staff or expatriates working in the countries you visit for the establishment of 'dumps' for spare tyres, tubes, brake blocks and other items likely to require replacement.

Before you do set off on such a journey, devote a substantial period of time to learning about the countries to be visited, their people and customs, terrain and routes (where they exist). Do not believe in the guide books and travel literature unreservedly. Seek out someone who has been there recently, and get a first-hand briefing on the current conditions. A grounding in the country's political affairs is important in avoiding inadvertent collision with authority, and possible subsequent incarceration. Gaols are seldom comfortable, and in some poorer states they are a very unfunny experience indeed! Simply pointing a camera in the wrong direction can be the beginning of a very unpleasant interlude, so check well in advance with the relevant authorities in the countries you visit. Sometimes you will need a permit to take photographs at all.

Obviously, the right time for this planning is well in advance of the trip, otherwise valuable time can be wasted simply trying to get into the country.

▶ ROUTE PLANNING AND MAPS ◀

If you think that all you have to do to plan a route is get hold of the appropriate map and draw a line, forget it. In the UK, maps are subject to inaccuracies regarding the status of rights of way, terrain can look very different to the way it appears on the map and features may have changed since the map was drawn. In less developed countries, maps should always be regarded with the deepest scepticism, and the user should be gratified if the general disposition of major geographical features is accurate.

For the mountain biker who intends to venture anywhere but the most carefully signposted routes, the ability to map-read is essential. More, it is part of the fun. The four golden rules which any expert will impress upon you (and which form the introduction of the excellent Ordnance Survey/*Daily Telegraph* publication, *Simply Map-Reading*, by Richard Neve) are:

- know exactly where you started from
- always check direction on moving off, and whenever you change it
- remember the scale
- read ahead.

These rules hold fast whether you are following clearly marked routes, roads or paths, or 'contouring', using the contour lines and relief features of the map to plot a navigable course in moorland or hills, where no routes exist.

The essentials of good navigation are simple. Know exactly where you are going, and use the map to help find viable routes and to anticipate the kind of terrain and surface you will encounter, the altitude to which you will have to ascend and the obstacles which you will encounter. Taking all these things into account, work out the likely duration of the journey. When you are a relatively experienced map-reader, you can make your calculations with ease, then monitor your trip with map, compass and watch, to make sure you are on course.

Map reading and navigation are skills which you should practise a few times in safe and predictable surroundings, before you attempt to lead a party across the slopes of Snowdonia in a fog. Be in possession of exactly the right sheet to cover the area of travel: if the planned route approaches the edge of the sheet, then take the adjacent one along as well. Understand scale, grid and key, for these are the features which bring the lines, symbols and colours to life and enable them to be related to the landscape before you. A reliable, tested magnetic compass, with lanyard, and the knowledge of how to use it, are essential; taking a spare in case of loss or damage is a very good idea.

The map is more than a coded plan of the route to follow. It's a way of assessing the factors which determine how you prepare and what you take. For instance, a route with a predominance of low, boggy ground, much running water and a lack of metalled paths will mean different tyres and pressures, gearing, water carriers and clothing from those you need on a route where high and rocky ground alternates with swift descents into dry scrubland or desert.

A map is also the only means by which you can be certain that the course you follow in practice is the one you have planned. Check position frequently, and plot your direction of travel in relation to clearly marked features or landmarks. Monitor your prog-ress against plan by comparing the time you actually take to cover a distance with the time you have allocated. Where the times differ significantly, the map provides the only safe way to adjust the route plan to arrive at your destination in time, or to retreat.

None of the skills of map reading is particularly difficult in itself, although there are a number of things to remember, and maps (and terrain) are infinitely variable. It's therefore misleading to attempt in this book a summary of the subject of map reading and navigation. However, some excellent and very simply written information is available in the form of Richard Neve's book and the larger *Mapstart* by Simon Catling, which is an introduction to the Ordnance Survey series of maps, and a first-rate step-by-step textbook. Buying both publications will set you back less than £7.00, and Richard Neve's book is the perfect size and weight for the pannier or large pocket.

The Crane Cousins on top of Kilimanjaro – truly an epic mountain bike expedition

Again, research is the only real answer for the mountain biker planning an expedition. If you want to be equipped with the best possible route information, the place to start is a good lending library. Write to or phone the Mountain Bike Club, Cross-country Cycling Club, Rough Stuff Fellowship and CTC, to request contacts and information about the area you wish to visit. In the library, persuade the librarian to make an index search on the area for you, and browse through everything which seems even vaguely relevant. This sort of detective work is absolutely fascinating, and a very enjoyable way of spending those winter days when even mountain biking is out of the question.

What you are looking for is every possible lead on previous visits and expeditions, so you can pick the brains of those who know about the practical difficulties. Naturally, you will visit High Commissions, embassies, tourist bureaux, but don't expect too much objectivity.

The purpose of all this information-gathering is to arrive at a position where you have sufficient data to:

- decide the goal of your journey
- understand the route to follow, its approximate duration and the major difficulties to be overcome
- choose the right time of year to travel with respect to weather, local festivals or points of interest, and availability of routes suiting mountain bikes

- understand the health risks and take sensible precautions in terms of inoculations and so on
- plan the equipment you till take
- prepare the machine for your journey
- meet the travel documentation requirements of all sovereign territories through which you will pass
- have some grasp of the main languages on your journey, so you are able to ask for the basics and show gratitude
- understand the non-physical obstacles, in order to avoid transgressing political or religious taboos, or giving offence by your behaviour or dress.

This by no means comprehensive list may seem daunting, but really does constitute the minimum preparation for any extended journey out of your own country. Much of it is common sense, but it is suprising how many people will set off with hardly any preparation at all, and just trust to luck.

Finally, read everything you can about other people's expeditions. The store of knowledge about such things is a bank of understanding and wisdom which will make your own trip far more enjoyable. Read the bibliography to find the books which contain little gems of know-how for the would-be bike trekker.

Mountain biking is a wonderful 'family' pursuit. The mountain bike could have been invented to bridge the cycling age gap. Fully equipped ,models are available with 24-inch wheels and a specification to match an adult 26-inch wheeler. The bikes are particularly strong on safety, and the very low gearing available allows the younger rider to tackle slopes that would be difficult on other machines. Apart from that, the appeal to the youngster of the ATB is obvious. The gearing and high-tech equipment make the bikes even more interesting than the BMX.

For the adult, one plus is that people don't feel they have to dress up to ride one. A sweater, jeans and trainers will do fine, whereas somehow the owners of the ten-speed drop-handlebar pseudo-racers which take such a significant share of the bike market seem to feel obliged to don special clothes every time they ride. The ATB is heralding in a more relaxed and universal approach to cycling, and some people who would never before have embraced cycling are using it as a route to fitness, incorporating road training for the children, and family fun.

If you have decided to make an investment in mountain bikes for your family, it would be as well to investigate a pursuit centre where you can hire bikes for the whole family, and try an easy ride together to see how you all take to it. If it goes well, it could be the forerunner of many a weekend exploring remoter parts of the country, or even travelling abroad on cycle tours.

▶ Planning for the youngest or weakest ◀

Organizing family riding is not easy. Other cycling groups tend to be riders of like ability, but a family will range across levels of skill and endurance; route selection, planning and leading the party are quite skilled tasks.

Naturally, the first thing to ensure is that all the riders have a modicum of proficiency, so as to avoid unnecessary

risk of accidents. A bad fall will not only spoil the day for you all, but in the case of a very young rider it may cause an aversion to riding for some time, so prepare the family well, and pay special attention to the training of the youngest. (Equally, you might find the adults in your party have trouble adjusting to the ATB.) Wherever your problems lie, don't discover them off-road, in a thunderstorm, ten miles from the nearest help. Pay particular attention to training and road safety, and if your local council or education authority run RoSPA cycling proficiency tests, make sure everyone takes them. Turn to the basic riding sections of this book, and get to the stage where all of you can ride as a safe, single unit. Whoever emerges as the natural leader must be aware of the strength and endurance of all the riders, and keep a watchful eye on them.

Leading cycling groups is often done just as well from the back, especially if the route is obvious, but the gradient steep. There is nothing more depressing in cycling than watching the main group get further and further away from you. People actually ride more strongly in the group than when they are trying to catch it up. It is possible to catch the rhythm and cadence of the other riders and overcome temporary fatigue. So ride with the weakest on hard sections to keep the group together.

Route pre-planning is vital. A reconnaissance by one or two of the family on a new route, especially in the early stages while you are all gathering experience, is a very good idea. If you know where the picnic place or cafe is, can anticipate the bits where difficulties might occur, or know where to find shelter if the weather changes, you are going a long way towards planning the perfect day, regardless of the weather.

Don't try to break endurance records when you're with your family. You are bound to hurt someone, or their pride, and it might be you! Family cycling is meant to be fun, and it certainly shouldn't be a competition. If planning for the youngest means that some members of the family still have excess energy at the end of a ride, and you happen to be camping, then we all know who rides to the farm for fresh water and other supplies.

Places to stay

The really committed family off-roaders will be camping, and immense fun that can be, if the planning has been impeccable. These days, it's virtually impossible to take pot-luck on camping sites in the UK, so you are far better advised to make one really comfortable site your base, and plan daily riding excursions. This has the advantage, in the better sites, of offering you plenty of alternatives to riding if you fancy a day out of the saddle. Another advantage will be that the family and bikes can be transported to the site by car, which means you can take a far larger and more comfortable tent than if you are restricted to the cycle panniers and racks for all your luggage.

Some families will prefer to swap the glamour of canvas (illusory unless the weather is perfect) for the comfort of the caravan, and the mountain bike is the perfect accessory for a caravan holiday. Hostels and pursuit centres are also excellent places to stay. The CTC will advise you on suitable family accommodation, and you are sure to meet many like-minded families, so you could even become part of a much larger group, if you choose. This allows riders of similar ability to stick together, and can be a good way to start a cycling friendship.

It is a sad fact that the average boarding house and hotel in the UK is 'not quite sure' about the cyclist. Motorists are always welcome, but there is a residual suspicion (in England especially) that cyclists are only cyclists because they want to do things on the cheap, and so they become less valued customers. Fortunately, this prejudice is less common outside the UK, and if you

seek the advice of the CTC you can be sure you will avoid contact with inhospitable innkeepers.

Feeding

Cyclists are burning up a lot of calories, especially off-road. Take plenty of protein for energy, but not in the form of vast meals. Eating too much at once can be quite dangerous, especially at breakfast time or lunch, leading to cramp, indigestion, heartburn and drowsiness. None of these will be good for your cycling. Eat four small and well-balanced meals a day rather then two or three big ones. Try to eat food which you know agrees with you, rather than setting out to sample new and exotic gastronomic delights. The combination of strange food, a different climate and extreme exercise can be deadly.

Breakfast should consist of fruit juice or fresh fruit, cereal with plenty of milk, as much toast and preserves as you need, and tea or coffee. Allow an hour before riding, and be sure to have full water bottles on the bike. **Water** is very important: if you have any doubts at all about the water supply, buy still mineral water and fill the bottles with that, either neat or flavoured with something like lemon barley.

It's a good idea to carry **snacks** on the bike, to keep up the level of blood sugar. Some like sweets; better is glucose (faster reaction; less harmful to teeth). A good complement to glucose are the health-food-type nut, cereal or fruit bars made by Jordans and others.

The type of **lunch** available will depend on whether you are using camping stoves, eating cold food you can carry, or planning the route to take in a food shop or café.

If you're cooking up for yourselves you are likely to be limited to one or two single burners. If so, be smart: cook healthy food, but conserve fuel and minimize washing up. Boil a pan of water and have some tea. Use the balance of the water to simmer a dehydrated vegetable soup, and eat that with cheese and healthy biscuits. Take frui as a dessert. This meal will provide all the energy you need, and it avoids excessive fat, which gives you stomach acid and makes for greasy pans. It's also quite variable, since you have a wide choice of meat- and vegetable-based soups, types of cheese and fruit. The equipment for cooking on the move like this takes up the minimum pannier space, and as long as some of the water bottles in the group have plain fresh water in them the food can be prepared at any time. It will give you no digestion problems and, as long as you don't over-indulge, you may ride off pretty soon after eating.

If you're lunching in a café, avoid greasy food. Salads are good, but only in areas where the mains water is to be trusted. (Salads are washed cold, so any germs in the water will be transferred to the salad.) Grilled fish will do you no harm, and nor will a burger, as long as it is not the 'sautéed in lubricant' kind; the prime consideration is not to over-eat or indulge in very rich or spicy foods if you have a hard afternoon's cycling in front of you.

Finally, with the day's strenuous exercise behind you, the **evening meal** can obviously be a more relaxed affair, with less restrictions on your intake.

Support vehicles

While cycling is a wholly self-sufficient pastime, it can often be enhanced by the judicious use of a support vehicle, to cut

Support vehicles can be anything from the family saloon with a roof-rack to this go-anywhere four-wheel-drive model

out the tedious bits of a journey – say the ride on public roads to the off-road course. This becomes an absolute necessity when you're transporting specially prepared racing machines and their riders to a race.

For the family group, the support vehicle is at its best as a comfortable temporary base camp, used to transport the group and machines to and from the day's ride, and as a safe haven, refreshment point and emergency first-aid post for bikes and riders. It follows that the well-equipped support vehicle will have carrying-points for two or more bikes, be large enough to accommodate all the riders and their gear, vital spares and food, and will ideally be sleepable in, if the occasion demands it.

It is up to you to decide to what extent you want to adapt the vehicle to its role, but if your pocket is deep enough, the choices are limitless. The writer uses a long-wheelbase four-wheel-drive machine of Japanese origin, which is almost perfect for the task of carting riders and machines to remote places. But the job can be almost as well done – though with rather less comfort – by almost any family car with roof- or boot-mounted bike carriers.

For family riding, the support car is a must unless you are lucky enough to live on the edge of perfect and legally accessible rough riding. And apart from the fact that it can be a bore to have to ride ten miles or more at dusk over crowded public roads, after you've used all your energy to ride twenty miles over rough terrain, it will mean that your bike will need lights and reflectors, and they add weight to an ATB that you can well do without. It is fine to ride the bike to the shorter and closer courses, but for anything longer, use a support vehicle, or travel by train.

British Rail has been heavily criticized in the 1980s for failing to cater for the cyclist. There are signs that this is now being rectified, at least on the more obvious country routes, and it is up to all cyclists to keep BR up to the mark, by patronizing the trains which do exist, and by complaining if the service is withdrawn. However, use your sense. Take a change of clothes along, and chuck a bucket of water over the bike before the return journey. The guard can be forgiven for refusing to allow you to transport half the Chilterns back to Marylebone on your bike and person!

You don't have to dress up in any particular type of clothing to enjoy mountain biking. On a machine with full weather protection in particular, you can just get on and ride. But if you insist on having no mudguards, regardless of weather, a black strip will rapidly adorn all your garments from the nape of your neck to the tip of your spine, with a fetching all-over accompaniment of little spatters of whatever was the prevailing soil on the last ride. While jeans, rugby shirts and sweaters are great for short runs, the keen rider will soon start thinking seriously about the correct kind of clothing to provide comfort, warmth and weather protection on longer rides, or for touring.

▶The Wrong materials◀

Although many riders improvise with jogging pants and sweat tops, with a waterproof nylon suit for rain, and a ski top for cold, these outfits aren't really satisfactory. Jogging pants may have the warmth, stretch and sweat absorbency, but once they're soaked by wet grass and nettles, they become baggy, clinging and uncomfortable, and all their good characteristics disappear. To persevere with such an uncomfortable garment in a climate where damp predominates won't do your long-term health any good either. To a macho few, this argues for shorts, but all-terrain riding is bound to drag you through nettles, brambles and other abrasive undergrowth at some time, not to mention the occasional tumble, and wearing leg protection is just common sense.

The popular sweat top is an excellent garment, and can be found in a variety of materials and weights, in long- and short-sleeved versions. Normally it is an indispensable part of the cyclist's wardrobe. However, once again mountain biking can pose particular problems. Pure nylon, proofed or unproofed, is not a satisfactory material for wearing to cycle any distance at all. It succeeds at keeping the rain out, but only at the cost

of promoting sweat and condensation on the inside, which will often saturate you more than if you had just ridden out the shower.

For shoes, the essential requirement is that the soles should be fairly stiff in order to transmit the power of the downstroke to the pedals, and not have any of it absorbed by the 'give' in both shoe sole and foot, which becomes painful after a while. Ordinary cycling shoes are rather frail for mountain biking, and the ventilated variety will mean a wet and squelchy foot in no time. Some kind of ankle protection is advisable, as is a means of securing the shoe laces, so that they don't get tangled in the transmission. Mountain bike boots and shoes are finding their way on to the UK market – regrettably at rather high prices as yet – but some types of trainer will do the job quite well.

▶The Right materials◀

So, what should the sartorially conscious mountain biker be looking for? Well, you need to be clear what kind of riding you will be doing. Some London mountain bikes never stray far from the Piazza in Covent Garden, and if posing is your priority, clothing will obviously play a big part. The newly emergent breed of bike couriers freely admit that bizarre clothing is part of their marketing act, and given that many of their clients are up-market ad agencies with ritzy premises and a high yuppie count on the staff, wild outfits are the business. Such figure-hugging finery can also be seen on the competition-minded rider (once the mud is scraped off), but, for once, the pose is not entirely non-functional. The materials from which some of these outrageous gladrags are wrought have a number of desirable properties.

Good cycling clothes must be temperature-tolerant – that is, the same outfit should, within reason, be cool in the hot and warm when it is chilly. This has

Custom-made clothing and touring equipment is available to suit all tastes

several virtues. First, in some touring conditions, for instance above the snow line in summer, the rider will be alternatively chilled and roasted as the route winds between shade and sunlight. In many latitudes, the temperature is extremely variable between midday and dusk. When you are on a proper cycle tour, it obviously makes good sense to be able to rely on as few garments as possible.

Garments should be fairly close-fitting, to avoid flapping in the wind, or filling with air, which creates wind resistance and causes undue skin cooling. Sweat should be absorbed away from the body quickly, and then evaporated from the garment at a controlled rate in order to maintain a normal body temperature. Hygiene dictates that cycling clothes need to be washed frequently, and therefore extremely fast drying is a priority. You also need this to make sure that the effects of a sudden shower are minimized. The insulating properties of the material should not be entirely lost when it is wet.

Additional virtues must include: durability of material to avoid wear through excessive washing and in the areas of maximum chafing; light weight and the ability to be packed into very small size so that a change of clothing can be taken on a trip without occupying too much space.

Fortunately, there are a lot of modern materials to complement the traditional cottons and wools which possess some of these attributes, and recent years have seen the emergence of some first-rate designers, manufacturers and retailers, specializing in smart, purpose-made clothing for cycling.

Lycra, both in polycotton and nylon, has proved a most versatile material for the cyclist. The nylon is good for shorts and long bottoms, possessing all the stretch, strength and fast-dry ability needed, while the polycotton is absorbent enough to be worn next to the skin, holds its shape well, can be produced in various weights and packs very small.

Polypropylene is a top-grade material for thermal underwear, and can be used in a number of weights, depending on conditions. Combined for heavier-weight bottoms, in a mix with other fabrics, it makes ideal cold-weather wear.

Goretex is the best waterproof material for active wear. It has many imitators, but few approach its quite amazing ability to waterproof the wearer completely without promoting excessive perspiration, whilst permitting condensation to migrate on the outside of the garment. Unfortunately, as tends to be the way with the best of anything, genuine Goretex is expensive, but it is well worth it.

A number of clothing suppliers specialize in cycling gear, not only with a wide variety of clothing for climatic conditions, but also in styles and colours enabling you to blend in with the terrain or, if you desire, to startle every sentient being within ten miles. The Swallow frames and cycle company has fairly recently gone into the clothing business in a comprehensive way; they offer a catalogue which is educational as well as a commercial. Madison Free-wheel have a range of clothing in their direct-mail service, and Rohan clothes− now becoming widely available − have some excellent items for mountain bikers.

Choice of clothing is a very personal matter, but since some basic recommendations may be useful for the beginner, here is a summary of what is suitable.

Clothing for Cold Conditions
Underclothes: 'Long johns' in polypropylene thermal material
Trousers: polypropylene mix
Socks: loopstitch cotton
Tops: medium-weight polycotton lycra, long-sleeved Goretex waterproof suit with hood
Ankleboot trainers with firm soles, or special Goretex mountain bike boots from Madison Freewheel (if budget allows)

Clothing for Warm Conditions
Underclothes: cotton-mix stretch briefs, polycotton singlet or T-shirt
Shorts or longs (depending on terrain): lightweight nylon lycra
Socks: as winter
Shoes: as winter
Tops: short-sleeved polycotton lycra lightweight, waterproof Goretex jacket with hood removed

Other clothing accessories which add measurably to comfort and safety include eye protection (ordinary sunglasses fall off, so properly designed sports glasses are better), mitts and gloves, and the all-important helmet.

Try on clothing before you buy. Uncomfortable cycle wear is not only going to look wrong, it can do you physical harm. Fortunately, many of the better cycle stores stock clothing, so you can sit on a bike wearing it and check whether you can reach the pockets and so on. The mail order houses perform a valuable service in the clothing area, and will usually have a wider range than most cycle shops.

One final hint for the cycle tourist − these modern fabrics are remarkably fast-drying, so if you take a polythene bag of washing or soap powder and hand wash your clothing overnight, you can save space and weight.

When it developed on the slopes of Marin County, mountain biking was a sport accessible to ordinary people. It remains so now. The only requirements are a mountain bike – a machine with tyres at least 1.5 inches wide, and the general description with which you will now be familiar – and the desire to pit wits, skill and strength against a punishing cross-country course with like-minded masochists!

To the credit of those in mountain biking who have influenced the development of racing, it has neither adopted rules that make it difficult for the beginner to line up alongside a seasoned professional rider, nor machines so sophisticated that they are beyond the reach of the average person. Indeed, at present, a standard Raleigh or Dawes gives a skilled rider just as much chance of success as machinery costing three times as much from Overbury or Cannondale. Long may this be the case. All too often, sports are 'captured' by the élitists, and the rules, equipment and skill factor of the event progress into realms which turn the rest of us into spectators. (Think of what happened to Go-Karting, which started as a genuine 'poor-person's' motor sport, and can now cost almost as much as Formula 3 to compete in.)

Of course, the same thing could happen to mountain biking, and as this book is written, there are undercurrents of politics in the ATB world, with its proponents seeking to develop in differing directions. Some manufacturers would like to see a greater concentration on organized national events with opportunities to attract big-name sponsorship; others, including figures prominent in the organization of present competitions, wish to preserve the sport's informality and freedom from regulation. Still others want to see the universality of competition preserved, but a regulatory competitive framework developed, to ensure that both big-name sponsored events – with manufacturers heavily involved – and competitions open to all can evolve.

The arguments are complex, and it is impossible at this stage to pre-judge an outcome. But the viewpoint of new and as yet latent mountain bikers might be that this sport sprang from the spontaneous urge to ride a rugged bike around rugged country in a spirit of freedom and pure enjoyment. All who seek to 'develop' competition should bear that in mind, and see that neither the costs, nor the challenges imposed upon would-be competitors, take it entirely beyond the scope of those of us of all ages who press our noses against cycle-shop windows and dream dreams.

▶COMPETITION◀

There are two main types of event for mountain bikers: long-course racing, and observed trials. Additionally, some cyclo-cross events allow participation from mountain bikes, although it has to be said that the ATB is not very competitive over this type of course.

Quite often, mountain bike racing takes the form of weekend rallies, in which both long-course and observed trials take place, with a spot of hill climbing and downhill slalom thrown in for good measure. These events can provide pleasure for riders of all abilities, and it is to be hoped that greater participation in the sport by manufacturers will encourage this format, rather than single Grand Prix-style long-course racing. It would certainly be in the interests of commercial trade sponsors to retain the rally-style event, for it provides a healthy breeding-ground for newcomers, and they are potential customers for bikes, clothing and other equipment.

Long-course racing

The first ever UK mountain bike race took place at a city-centre cycle track in London in 1984. It wasn't until 1988 that the Mountain Bike Club and Shimano UK got together to stage the 'Shimano Trail' series of long-course events around the country. The series lasted six months with one event a month, and although it suffered from organizational teething problems unavoidable for such an ambitious undertaking in a new sport, it gave competition experience at national level to many riders.

Courses varied from a twenty-five-mile single-loop track in Scotland to a two-mile circuit in the West Midlands, and the events attracted a field so large and varied that by the end of the season, arrangements were under way for establishing new classifications. Now mountain bike events cater for riders under sixteen and over forty, for women-only racing and for novice, 'sport' and expert riders.

Long-course racing in the UK is modelled on the two World Championships held each year in the USA and Europe, where British riders are not entirely unknown. For many years the UK racers were in awe of their American counterparts and nobody thought that a British mountain biker stood a chance in world competition. Then, in 1988, things began to change as several cyclo-cross riders started to supplement their winter racing with summer mountain biking. Their all-round skills soon began to give them an edge, and they started winning all the major races, raising standards significantly throughout mountain biking. At the Mountain Bike World Championships in Switzerland, a UK cyclo-cross rider, Tim Gould, finally put the UK on the world mountain bike map when he came third, beating US star John Tomac.

Performances like Gould's, coupled with the establishment of competitive national events such as the Shimano Trail, will have three major areas of impact on the direction of sport in the UK, if they are properly nurtured.

First, foreign competitors will come here to try the mettle of our best riders, and more British aspirants will receive vital 'blooding' in competition.

Second, new competitions will spring up, supplementing the Shimano event, and stimulating further interest all over the country. Already, the 'Arena Trophy', to be run in the spring of 1989, is

mooted by The Arena Press, the publishers of the *Mountain Biking Handbook*, and the sleeping giant of television is at last beginning to wake up to this sport.

Third, media interest will be generated, leading new entrants into the sport and creating increased pressure for countryside access for mountain bikers, as well as a need for some central administration to deal with the interests – sporting and non-sporting – of mountain bikers everywhere. It will be interesting to see the people who take on this task, and how they will cope with it.

At the time of writing, those wishing to take part in long-course racing need only to turn up at a race and present themselves to the starter, with a suitable bike in good mechanical order. Inevitably, as the sport becomes more popular, it will have to be more organized, and already the various magazines are beginning to pre-notify events and publish entry forms, sometimes with an entry fee. *Making Tracks* offers a good reader service in listing the various competitions taking place all over the country, and it is encouraging to see that the numbers of events are steadily increasing. You would be well advised to join a club locally it you're interested in racing regularly; the Mountain Bike Club will put you in touch with the nearest group of fellow-sufferers.

▶*Observed trials*◀

This fascinating and more relaxed branch of the sport has been around for rather longer than long-course racing, with the first UK event taking place at Heaton Park, Manchester in 1981. Because the riders compete essentially against themselves over a marked-out course of varying difficulty, there is less physical risk involved, but skill levels are still satisfyingly high. Trials have the added advantage that age poses no difficulty and adds no limits.

An observed trials course may be quite an extended cross-country route,

Hill climb

taking in any number of obstacles and hazards which the rider has to negotiate. Sections of the course are observed by scrutineers, and penalty points are awarded against the rider for such things as touching down with a foot or both feet, or coming to a halt. Refusing a section and coming off not surprisingly incur the highest penalties.

The pure observed trial event usually takes place on a fairly small track of hilly woodland. This allows spectators to move from section to section freely, and you certainly see much more of the event than you do watching a long-course race from a fixed position.

A longer version of the observed trial is an 'Enduro' or time and observation trial. These are conducted either round a circuit or on a point-to-point basis, and can be as long as 30 miles. The 'Enduro' combines the factors of endurance and timed performance through a series of sections with observed skills, and it makes for varied and interesting competition. Whereas the riders in the observed trial have time to examine each section before competing, in the 'Enduro' they compete against the clock, and have to take the next section regardless of the fact that the rider in front may still be trying to get away from a gooey bit! Competitors do all walk the course prior to competing, so it pays to arrive early.

Some riders like to adapt the bike to the course, not just by removing mudguards, bottles and so on, but by taking off surplus chainwheels – and often the changer mechanism itself, if the terrain suggests that the smaller ring alone will be needed. It makes a lot of sense to do this well before the event, but only when you've got an idea of the course. If you're unsure whether high ratios will be required – for instance for a downhill slalom – leave the transmission mods till race day.

Hill climbs and downhill slalom are events in themselves. Indeed, the latter is what the mountain bike was originally developed for. Because of the lack of long, dry downhill routes in the UK, the downhill is now a feature of the event rather than the event itself, but this doesn't mean that there is a dearth of challenging (some might say desperate) descents, rather that they are over more quickly than the Californian variety. The annual 'Wendover Bash' in Buckinghamshire combines all the disciplines of mountain bike competition in a weekend of trials over a Forestry Commission course in the Chilterns, and it has a descent which, while negotiable by beginners (when dry), can become truly spectacular when a less sensitive soul eschews the brakes and lets it all hang out. A hump at the end of the tortuous downhill dash causes ever larger bits of daylight to intrude between rider and terra firma as the limits get pushed out, with the inevitable result that some bikes and riders tend to finish the course with what has become known as 'wipe-out'!

Hill climbing is a sort of self-imposed twentieth-century version of the Inquisition, to judge by the distorted expressions of the riders who proceed slowly by, their mouths where their ears should be, eyes popping with the effort of it all, pursued closely by observers, there to record the very inch where machine and rider collapse to the ground with all the grace and anguish of a gut-shot bear. Scorecards are provided, and it is up to the individual riders to ensure that they are filled out accurately after each section, so that the complex deductions – involving penalties, times and performances over the many sections – can be completed and compared to find the placing riders.

Another competitive aspect of the sport is mountain bike orienteering, which tests navigational skills as well as performance, and is an ideal 'family' event, enabling riders of all skill levels to take part and enjoy themselves to the full.

Even this early in the development of the sport, events are beginning to attract reasonable prizes, with ATBs, equipment and clothing put up by manufacturers and retailers; and with the emergence of professional and semi-professional teams, sponsored by some of the leading marques, the spectre of cash prizes may soon rear its head. Currently, ATB sport has something for riders of all ages and skills. At the risk of repetition, it would be a pity if those at the head of the sport lost sight of this universal appeal in the rush to attract big money and media attention.

The author gratefully acknowledges the help of Max Gluskin of the Mountain Bike Club, and Geoff Apps of the Cross-Country Cycling Club, in preparing this section.

SELF - SUFFICIENCY

This book is not the place for an extensive summary of first-aid techniques. However, certain injuries are fairly common in off-road mountain biking, and this section gives a few tips, with reminders on how to distinguish the minor injury from one which should be taken more seriously.

With regard to **simple cuts and grazes**, plasters and bandages have two functions: to stop bleeding and keep the dirt out. Where possible, leave a cut or graze to the open. Bandages create a warm moist environment in which bacteria proliferate. To minimize this, use an antiseptic – one of the most useful is povidone iodine, which can be obtained from chemists in a dry-powder spray can.

Blisters are best anticipated and avoided. If you do get them, second best is to cover them and leave them alone. If they burst, then the whole of the raised skin should be excised, at a convenient time, with a pair of scissors sterilized by boiling. If you don't do this, by leaving the covering flap of dead skin with its hole in one corner you are asking for infection to enter and delay healing.

Deep cuts that have a degree of pulsatile spurting indicate arterial involvement. The flow from the artery can be very alarming, but it must be controlled. Tourniquets are now regarded as being the cause of more harm than good. You should apply pressure on a pulse point above the wound. If you find, in applying a dressing to the wound, that blood is still seeping through, add a further dressing on top. Don't keep removing the pad as this disturbs the clotting processes.

A **sprain** describes the rupture of a few of, or all, the fibres in a ligament. Ligaments are bands of toughened tissue; several ligaments strap across each joint to stop it falling to pieces. Sprains are best dealt with by a cold compress and supportive bandaging. (Elasticated tubing is ideal, as it doesn't wriggle loose.) Witch hazel in the compress is as useful as anything, but cold water is perfectly adequate. It is acceptable to walk on a sprained ankle, but you should keep movement at the ankle joint to a minimum. Fibres in one of the ligaments have been broken, and the less you move it, the sooner healing can take place.

Tendinitis describes a condition which takes place when a tendon is subjected to excessive and repeated unusual activity. The tendon becomes chafed within the sheath which surrounds it. In cycling it is particularly important with respect to the setting of the handlebars. The riding up and down of the wrists, if they are at an awkward angle, can bring on an immensely painful tendinitis at the wrist. Treatment for this can eventually require hydrocortisone injection or surgical release of the tendon. Initially immobilization and rest of the affected part, with or without an anti-inflammatory such as ibuprofen (Neurofen), is the best approach.

Moving on to the heavier problems, **fractures** are usually obvious. The quartet of signs are pain, deformity, swelling and inability to move the affected joint, though not all of these occur with every fracture. Bruising is a later symptom, and a significant degree of bruising can draw attention to a fracture in a small bone, where you might previously have thought you had a sprain. Beware of presuming a sprain of the thumb. Fracture of the little bone under the hollow at the base of the thumb (the scaphoid) can be difficult to diagnose, and it will certainly present future problems. Advice for most fractures is obvious: immobilize the affected area and go to a hospital. If there is difficulty in moving one or all limbs and this is associated with any degree of concussion or neck injury, the injured party must not be moved until experienced personnel are on hand to protect any possible damage to the spinal cord.

With respect to **chest injuries**, it is

worth pointing out that many hospital casualty departments do not take X-rays of a simple broken rib (one where there is no impairment of breathing), as treatment for this is the same as for bruising, that is, simple analgesia.

Dislocations are best left to the experienced. Remembering a John Wayne film does not count as experience.

Collapses as far as the limits of this book are concerned, must be treated with common sense. Don't feed drinks to someone who has collapsed. If the circulation is busy coping with the supply of blood to the muscles, the supply to the stomach is limited. Copious mugs of fluid are going to lie in a collapsed person's abdomen, making him or her queasy. Fluids must not be given to anyone who might need surgery. The single most important requirement in a case of unconsciousness is to preserve the airway. If necessary, put a finger in the person's mouth and make sure that the tongue is forward and has not been swallowed.

The author is grateful to Dr Alistair Reece, MB, CHB, for help in preparing this section.

Mountain bikes are pretty tough, but that does not mean that they will struggle on for ever without being afforded the basic minimum of attention. The proud boast *I never touch the bike, just chuck a bucket of water over it from time to time* indicates a rider to whom one should give a wide berth. One day that rider will reach for the brakes and they won't be there.

All the same, the ATB is a low-maintenance machine in normal use, and attention to a few essentials on a regular basis, together with the knowledge of when to ask an expert for help, will keep the wheels turning reliably for many thousands of miles. Not everyone wishes to become an engineer, so we have divided this section into those tasks which any novice should be able to perform, those requiring greater expertise and those things best left to the dealer.

▶SADDLES◀
Novice

Most modern saddles require no adjustment, but there is one notable exception; a Brooks-type leather saddle, such as the B17. This has a hexagonal nut under the peak (nose) of the saddle, which tensions a threaded bar, whose function is to take up any slack in the leather seat itself. This nut is reached by an open-ended spanner of the appropriate size, and can be moved in a series of quarter-turns.

The pure leather saddle ought to be proofed with saddle soap or Neats foot oil, to keep it supple and weatherproof. This is very important on an ATB with no mudguards, as much spray and other gunge ends up under the saddle, so don't miss the underneath when you're proofing.

Seat position adjustments are made either by releasing the QR lever on the seat clamp and lifting or lowering the seatpin, or by using the appropriate size

of Allen key to slacken the mechanism of the micro-adjusting clamp to alter tilt, or to slide the saddle forward and back. Never use an Allen key or spanner which is not a snug fit on the nut, bolt or grub screw to be tightened, and always remember to re-tighten whatever you loosened in order to adjust. On the older Brooks-type saddles, micro-adjusters could not be fitted, so the old-fashioned seatpin, connected to the saddle with a ring clamp and nuts, will be in use. You can use a straightforward box spanner on this.

Expert

Expertise is really only required here if there is some problem, such as the saddle becoming difficult to shift. Do not heave away at it. All you will do is etch zig-zags into the seatpin, which on light alloy can create the potential for a future breakage, and if that happens at speed in rough country, the results can be unpleasant. Ease the grip of the seat lug by removing the QR assembly altogether and *gently* prizing the two sides apart with a hard wood wedge. Only microscopic movement should be required before the pin begins to move.

Dealer

If the above methods don't solve the problem, then the pin has become corroded in, or it is an oversized one, forced in in the first place. Don't attempt any further surgery – take it in to your dealer, who will have special tools.

▶BARS, STEMS AND GRIPS◀
Novice/Expert

The adjustment routine for stems and bars is described on pages 75–8. Very little maintenance of these items is required, although the stem on at ATB is often involved in the front-brake control

Adjusting the front changer

cable operation. This means that you will have to check that the cable is properly routed after you make any brake adjustment. Either cables are led into a large-diameter hole on top of the stem, with the inner cable alone emerging from a smaller hole in the bottom and travelling on down to where it meets the cantilever harness; or a pulley-type device is used. If you have the pulley-type system, check from time to time that the pulley is running freely.

Bars should not pose any problems once they are fitted in the correct position. Alloy-to-alloy bar-stem combinations can creak, but this is not usually a sign of distress, unless it is accompanied by movement. If the movement can't be corrected by careful tightening (not over-tightening), see your dealer.

Grips can wear out under really excessive use, although within reason wear only makes the better types more comfortable. Too much scraping along the ground does tend to accelerate the end of a grip, and there is no alternative to cutting it off with a sharp knife at that stage. Use a good glue for the replacement.

Dealer

As ever, if the stem has become stuck in the head tube or the bars cannot be held firm in the stem, it falls to the unfortunate dealer to straighten out the mess.

▶PEDALS◀
Novice

It is as well to pay a fair amount of attention to pedals. One pair sports four ball-race-type bearings (usually), and these are down among the muck a lot of the time. Although the bearings are sealed on most good makes, you should spin and listen to them to make sure that they are revolving sweetly. Pulling and pushing will indicate slack bearing adjustment or wear.

Expert

Rough-running or slack pedals should be attended to at the earliest opportunity, as they have a cleverly designed gremlin built in, which knows exactly when you have reached your remotest point from home, and hardens the whole assembly up as if it was running in concrete!

Remove the pedal from the crank, employing a carefully judged tap from a hammer to the body of the spanner if the pedal is reluctant to move. Remember that turning the pedal in the direction of revolution when you are on the bike will tighten it up, for fairly obvious reasons, and don't spend half the afternoon tapping with a hammer to tighten it! (To do so will certainly result in a trip to the dealer, and could mean a new crank as well.) Placing the pedal thread in a vice, with the screw thread protected from the jaws, undo the dust cap of the pedal to gain access to the bearings, and unscrew. Some pedals will have cassetted bearings, some cone and balls. Replace any worn components with proprietary spares from the same stable, packed in the recommended grease or lubricant. Re-tighten only until there is no play and the pedal revolves sweetly. Replace all lock nuts and washers, making sure that everything is spotless, replace the dust cap and refit the pedal to the bike. Check adjustment some 30 or 40 miles after refitting.

Dealer

If you lack the confidence to perform the above, or the pedal is bent and you suspect the crank may also be damaged, get your dealer to have a look as soon as possible. Damaged pedals are uncomfortable to ride with and should be repaired or replaced quickly.

▶WHEELS◀

Novice

Unless you're an expert, your wheel maintenance will really be restricted to vigilance. Watch the tyre wear, check running pressures, remove stones and thorns, and repair punctures. Plastic tyre levers should be used to lever tyre beads over the edge of the rim, allowing you to get your fingers in to remove the rest of the tyre and gain access to the tube. Mountain bike punctures are seldom subtle affairs, and the hole is usually obvious. If it isn't, use a bucket of water to locate the bubbles, dry and clean the tube well in the region of the hole, apply the solution and don't attempt to place the patch until the solution is dry. Often it is advisable to put a strip of spare tubing between tube and outer if the hole is large; then replace the outer cover as soon as possible. You will learn to refit the cover with just your fingers after a while, and this is good technique, as it avoids further punctures from crimping the tube with the tyre levers.

A wheel jig is essential for spoke-tensioning and wheel-building

Expert

Wheels are works of art, and their adjustment is best not experimented with. If rims become kinked or buckled or spokes lost, they should be attended to quickly. Spoke replacement, wheel trueing, even wheel-building can be done by the amateur, but they require the right equipment – a good wheel-building jig can be obtained from Madison Freewheel – and some training or advice from an experienced amateur or professional wheel-builder is essential, as is the use of a proper spoke spanner. Good books on the subject are available. *Richard's Bicycle Book* deals with basic maintenance, spoke-tightening and correcting minor kinks, and an American

publication, *Building Bicycle Wheels* by Robert Wright, covers the whole topic.

For novice and expert alike, any deflection of the rim of more than a half-inch should be taken to the dealer, since it is easy to cause irreparable damage to an expensive alloy rim through inexperience. If you are fascinated by the idea of wheel-building, read the books, and hang around your nearest specialist friendly dealer; often they will pass on tips to a sufficiently interested and dedicated bike nut, and you will be learning one of the few genuine engineering skill remaining in an electronic world.

Hubs are a similar proposition to pedals, although increasing production quality in sealed bearing manufacture means they give longer service before attention to the bearings is needed. However, it can never be ruled out altogether, given the life led by a well-used ATB, and frequent checks to ensure smooth running and lack of play make sense. Bearing change and relubricating procedures are the same as those for pedals in principle; most manufacturers include good working drawings with the original item, although these will not have come with a complete bike. A sympathetic dealer will advise, or take on the job for you. If you want to learn, ask to watch – you may have to wait for a convenient time, but it is worth it to learn a wrinkle or two.

▶TRANSMISSIONS◀
Novice/Expert

The limit to sensible mucking-about with expensive derailleur systems, both front and rear, is indicated by the adjustment screws provided for the owner to alter sideways movement of the arm which shifts the chain to higher or lower cogs or chainwheels. Tightening the control cable to take up the stretch inevitable in early use is also reasonable. Even these adjustments should be undertaken only after consulting bike or manufacturer's handbook or dealer, so you know that you select the correct screw to effect the direction of movement you desire.

For the novice, it is preferable to err on the side of caution when adjusting these screws, since too coarse a 'tweak' can deposit the chain in the rear wheel, or tuck it firmly down between chainwheels and bottom-bracket. Today's chains are not the robust affairs they were in the days before six- and seven-speed blocks, and ham-fisted work in this area is a false economy. Let the expert do the job.

Having said that, if you are prepared to go to the expense of equipping yourself with a proper bike workstand, which supports the frame while you make delicate but observable adjustments on the running derailleur, then you can carry out first-rate work. Transmission tuning is one of those tasks which really is rendered hundreds of times easier with the right tools. Trying to work on the gears with the bike upside down is a fool's errand – it leads to poor adjustment at best, and badly mangled fingers at worst.

A golden rule for all mountain bikers is to look after the entire transmission system by cleaning it regularly. After *every* cross-country ride, brush the chain to remove all grit. You can obtain special brushes for the job, which completely encircle the chain and have an integral pressurized dispenser for a non-greasy spirit-based lubricant, which really is a great improvement on the black syrup of a few years back. While expensive to purchase, this device will make back its cost many times over in enhanced chain wear. Clean the chainwheels with one toothbrush, and use another to dislodge caked-on mud and grit from the exposed cable runs and pulleys.

Dealer

If you can't make the improvements you need within the normal scope of adjustment built into the mechanisms, and you have checked the cables for correct tension, and they are neither too loose nor too tight, then suspect a distorted fork end or a bent mechanism, and go to the dealer.

The best way for the rider to adjust cables is using the screw tensioners in the thumb shifters, but if the indexed mechanism for gear selection has become worn, gear selection will become less precise, and no amount of fiddling with cable tension will help for long. New shifters are indicated, unless you are prepared to switch the lever provided to the friction shift position and have done with it.

Very occasionally, braze-on cable shifters can get knocked off, and if that happens, nothing can be done with the gears. This must be attended to by a dealer, and will entail re-brazing, checking the frame for weakness, and re-spraying, at least in the area of the repair if the paint can be matched – and possibly you will need a complete re-spray if it can't.

▶BRAKES◀
Novice

The security of all bolts, free working of all moving parts, tension of cables, play in levers and wear of brake blocks should be checked very regularly. It is not going too far to check them before every journey.

When brake blocks and alloy rims are new, they will be very noisy. After a few miles, everything wears itself in nicely and braking becomes progressive and powerful. If it does not, suspect grease deposits or some other kind of contamination on the rims. Give them a good wipe with methylated spirits, then polish clean, using a soft rag with nothing on it. Check the alignment (see page 38), and if that doesn't work, consult a dealer. Change brake blocks regularly, using snug-fitting tools, and purchase only the best composite blocks (Aztec, or the type recommended by the brake manufacturer).

Expert

Special tools are available for the rider

Tensioning the cable of the rear changer

Brake adjustment

who wants to keep brakes at the peak of their performance at all times, and anyone who regularly rides fast over mountainous terrain will require this kind of assurance. Their function is to hold cantilevers and U-brakes in precise position while minute adjustments are made, and minimize the amount of bad language needed by the fitter. You can also get tools for cable cutting and adjustment.

Dealer

If brake components don't work correctly when they are properly adjusted, then something more fundamental is responsible. Bent braze-ons can cause problems, and cantilevers and brake arms can become distorted under exceptionally heavy loads, and these will require replacement. It is not worth risking fatigue in a braking component – coffins are more expensive than brake assemblies. Go to the dealer if you can't get your brakes up to scratch by normal adjustment or replacement of blocks.

FRAMES
Dealer

There is nothing that even the expert amateur should attempt on a frame, except changing the headset and bottom-bracket bearings. Again, for this you need the right tools, including a comprehensive set of specialized spanners and extractors (which will depend on the manufacture of the bearing), and a proper bike-support frame to hold everything steady, without inflicting damage to thin frame tubes. These are expensive items to use on just one bike, infrequently, and they are really only economic in group or club ownership.

The Mountain Bike Club does have a club workshop, which is fine if you live in the Telford area, but for this type of work, you will do best to go to your dealer or frame-builder.

Worn bottom-brackets or headsets can be easily diagnosed. The bottom-bracket starts clicking and graunching. The headset allows the fork to move when braking, and you can't adjust the fork without the steering binding. Both these faults render the machine uncomfortable to ride, and should be rectified fast.

A more basic (and expensive) frame problem is impact or overload damage causing distortion and misalignment. If this is bad enough to see with the bike in riding trim, it is serious. If there's no visible damage to frame joints – such as paint cracking or strained joints – it is possible the frame can be jig-straightened, but if the joints are strained, a rebuild or new frame is indicated.

CLEANING

Perhaps the single most important contribution to the maintenance of a mountain bike is keeping it clean. There are those who would have you believe that it is macho to have a mud-caked iron, and all that you need is to dunk it in the odd bog from time to time to shift the topsoil. Such neglect will lead to bearing trouble faster than bad lubrication. Keep your bike clean, especially around moving parts. Use the new spirit-based lubricants which do not attract grit and dust, and keep the bike out of the rain, and you will get by with the minimum of spanners.

The reasons why riders design their own machines vary from the strictly practical, such as being unable to find a frame that is sufficiently comfortable, to pure élitism, and the desire to own something completely unique.

Oddly enough, for a sport which seems to attract its fair share of individuals, there is little individuality about most mountain bike frames. The vast majority of affordable designs are very similar, with the notable exception of the Highpath, and the new 'Dingbat' – a sort of trials Highpath with a lot of pedigree – and some of the new carbon-fibre exotica, whose price tends to eliminate most mountain bikers, however much they want a unique machine.

One the other hand, the fact that we will probably all end up with pretty similar machines, the finer points of which can only be appreciated by other enthusiasts, seems not to deter the rider who is set on a bespoke bike. What that rider gains is a quality of build unobtainable in the normal production-run set-up. Firms such as Swallow, Overbury and many of the other established frame-builders specialize in the ATB's sell-on quality, and all show a readiness to meet the customer's demand in terms of measurements and brazed-on bits for running gear and accessories.

In the main, frame-builders will have developed a range of frames for differing purposes, and will not expect the rider to specify a bike which differs too fundamentally from one of their basic designs. This is because the builders usually know full well what they are doing, and are not prepared to allow their very good reputation to be tarnished by someone else's ill-informed experiment. This doesn't mean that there is no room for individual choice. Frames can be specified in a range of steel alloys (or even aluminium) to give differing ride characteristics. They can be built lugged or lugless, with sloping or straight top tubes, oval or round main frame members, or a mixture; they can have various arrangements for connecting seat stays and seat tube, different front-fork types, and a plethora of braze-ons. The varieties of finish available are almost infinite, and of course equipment is developing at a rapid pace – although there appear to be only two viable ATB gear sets at the time of writing.

The point to remember, if you decide to go for a tailor-made bike, is that the people who build bikes have a lifetime's experience, and you can either benefit from it, or totally ignore it. If you choose the latter course, then you may as well walk blindfold into the nearest cycle shop and ask for a mountain bike – it is just as silly, but you will only be wasting your own time. If you are prepared to spend the £400-plus that a handmade frame will cost – and you *can* spend considerably more – then listen to the builder, and learn why things are designed and made in a certain way. Let the builder draw out from you the use to which the bike will be put, and the terrain over which it is likely to be ridden. Don't be dogmatic about size until you have been measured properly, and listen to the builder's opinion on your equipment choice.

So, what tangible benefits are you getting by going 'handmade'? Well, specialist frame-builders of repute will not just be welding together other people's bits to your specification. Indeed, the best ones won't be welding at all – they will concentrate on methods of construction which do not detract from the strength of join as does welding. Lugged brazing or, even better, lugless brazing will prevail, which means that lower temperatures are used and an extra fillet of brazing material is crafted to form a smooth joint, stronger and lighter than with lugged construction, and several times less likely to fracture than a welded one.

Most production mountain bike frames are welded, since it is a far faster way of building than lugless brazing.

The 'Dingbat' – a highly specialized trials machine, built to individual specification

The consequent restriction on the strength of the joints means manufacturers have to use heavy butting in the frame tubing, adding weight.

Custom-builders often make their own frame components, such as bottom-brackets, so that they can both achieve the geometry they have designed for their creations, and avoid the crimping and bending of fragile, tapering seat and chainstays to which less expensive machinery is subjected, to make components fit. Often, a custom frame is designed not only for a rider, but for a specific rear hub, chainset and clearance for a certain tyre size, and this has to be accomplished without butchery of frame tubes. The resulting frame often looks more fragile than its production-built counterpart, but in reality is many times more resilient.

Two renowned and excellent custom-building firms have been named in this section, but they are not the only ones. Really good hand-builders don't proliferate, however, as any of them will tell you, it is not a recipe for an early retirement to a tax haven, and the apprenticeship is long and hard. Equally, not everyone who builds frames by hand is doing a wonderful job. Start with the ads in the cycle mags, ask friends who have had frames built, send away for literature and look at the way firms do business. The good makers will not promise to fit you up in a week. They will want to see you and talk about your requirements. Some will be relatively large organizations, others will be just one person. If they are worth their hire, they will show you samples of their work and introduce you to other customers for an independent opinion.

The bike of the future? A lightweight but ultra-stiff carbon-fibre/Kevlar frame

With this rhetorical question, there is no single answer that does not pose further questions. Without a doubt, the tough little fat-tyred straight-handlebar bike has had a tremendous impact on the world of cycling in the late 1980s. Sales have increased beyond the manufacturers' wildest expectations, people never before drawn to cycling have become keen cyclists, and new businesses and industries based entirely on mountain bikes have developed. If nothing else were to happen, the achievements to date would still be startling. It's as if the whimsical desire to ride a bike as fast as possible down a back-country Californian firebreak were a fundamental urge in all of us, and all over the world! Of course, that *is* pure whimsy, and the economist would probably have a perfectly sound explanation for why a declining industry was suddenly transformed by a bike that really wasn't that different to what was already on offer!

In the end, the reasons for the mountain bike boom are not all that important. The fact is, mountain *biking* (in all its manifestations) is now bigger than mountain *bikes*, and it is a positive force which can be encouraged in order to give healthy and harmless fun to people of all ages, encourage an industry which has environmental as well as commercial benefits, and provide a way of getting people to value and care for the countryside, wherever they live and ride.

If this is to happen, all involved would do well to recognize the part they have to play. First, the riders of mountain bikes, whether they are seekers after solitude, downhill racers, commuters, urban couriers or just people having fun. The bike is unique, it consumes nothing, costs relatively little and can

confer more pleasure than almost any other form of transport. Used badly, though, it can endanger the rider, pedestrians and other traffic, compromise the enjoyment of other country users, scare horses, spoil crops and damage wild plants. If mountain bikers remember this, they can avoid making cycling synonymous with hooliganism and foolhardiness. Over the years, cyclists have built up a reputation for being responsible folk – it would be sad if the vast increase in their number destroyed that well-earned respect.

Second, the people who organize and channel the sport of mountain biking should reflect on the wide range of adherents which the new bike has brought into the cycling world, and make sure that it continues to offer excitement and achievable challenges to all. There should be a sustained effort to improve access to the country routes the bike is designed to ride, as well as to set up a framework of competition. Not everyone wants to race, and the bike is designed to go slow as well as fast.

Third, those who are involved in the marketing activity which builds sales for the manufacturers of bikes, accessories, clothing and other items could resist the temptation to turn mountain biking into just another hyped-up thrill for the super-rich, super-fit super-young. This applies to media and industry alike. The wide franchise achieved by the ATB indicates that a lot of people looked at the product and said 'This makes sense' – not 'Fine, but let's make it more extreme'. If product development stopped entirely, sales would not drop away, and indeed it might give the trade time to consolidate and to develop the accessory range for existing models, in order to attract an even wider public, which would in turn broaden and enrich the base. The tendency to produce second- and third-generation machinery, ever more extreme, before the potential for the first, highly successful range of mountain bikes has been explored, is hard to understand, and it may discourage rather than attract. The bike is a multi-purpose tool, and racing is only one use.

Finally, the administrators – not just in the sport of cycling, but in local authorities, politics, transport planning, economic forecasting – need to take a good look. People are 'getting on their bikes'. This is good for health, public expenditure, conservation of vital resources, traffic movement, and probably inflation, the balance of payments and the common cold. Administrators can encourage it by building more and better facilities for cyclists, deterring motorists from careless behaviour towards cyclists by more severe penalties, and asking cycling bodies to take part in the growing debate about countryside use.

So, whether your terrain is the slopes of Snowdonia or the cobbles of Covent Garden, enjoy mountain biking, and help others to enjoy it too.

▶BIBLIOGRAPHY◀

Richard Ballantine, *Richard's Bicycle Book* (Pan)

Simon Catling, *OS Mapstart* (Collins Longman Atlases)

Nicholas Crane, *Cycling in Europe* (Pan)

       The Great Bicycle Adventure (Oxford Illustrated Press)

Martyn Forrester, *The Survival Skills Handbook* (Sphere Books)

John Franklin with RoSPA, *Cyclecraft* (Unwin Paperbacks)

Ian Lynn *et al*, *The Off-road Bicycle Book* (Leading Edge Press and Publishing)

Richard Neve, *Simply Map-Reading* (Telegraph Publications)

Bettina Selby, *Riding the Desert Trail* (Chatto and Windus)

Rob Van Der Plas, *The Mountain Bike Book* (Bicycle Books, San Francisco)

Annabel Whittet with Pamela D. Stewart, *The Bridleways of Britain* (Whittet Books)